Anselm of

Sister Benedicta Ward read
Manchester and theology at th
numerary Fellow of Harris Manchester College, she teaches
Church History and Spirituality for the Faculty of Theology at
the University of Oxford and is the Reader in the History of
Christian Spirituality, with special interest in the Desert Fathers
and Anglo-Saxon spirituality. Sister Benedicta is a member of
the Anglican religious community of the Sisters of the Love of
God, and has written a number of books on early monasticism
and aspects of the Middle Ages.

ANSELM OF CANTERBURY

His Life and Legacy

Benedicta Ward SLG B.A. D.Phil.

First published in Great Britain in 2009

Society for Promoting Christian Knowledge
36 Causton Street
London SW1P 4ST

British Library Cataloguing-in-Publication Data
A catalogue record for this book is available from the British Library

ISBN 978–0–281–06104–4

1 3 5 7 9 10 8 6 4 2

Typeset by Graphicraft Ltd., Hong Kong
Printed in Great Britain by Ashford Colour Press

Produced on paper from sustainable forests

To 'those who love me, and whom I do most truly love'
the living and the dead

Contents

Acknowledgements

I want to thank all those who have discussed the content of this study with me and the friends I have made in doing it, in Italy and North America as well as in Oxford and London. I have been encouraged and enabled in this work by many people: in Canterbury, in the library, the archives and the cathedral; in London, at the British Library and by my editors at SPCK; in Oxford, in Bodley, and by colleagues and friends in my two colleges, Harris Manchester and St Stephen's House; in the Theology faculty by my friends and students; above all, by my patient sisters who gave me support and space for this work.

I have been especially aided in writing this book by the memory of the unfailing inspiration and training given me by Sir Richard Southern, the greatest Anselmian of all. My first book (*Prayers and Meditations of St Anselm with the Proslogion*) was done at his suggestion and with his wise guidance; in this book I have drawn constantly on his work, hoping always that he has been guiding me with more than one astringent 'yes, but . . .'.

This book is offered as a memorial of Anselm, nine hundred years after his death, with living affection and continued response.

Benedicta Ward SLG

1

Who was Anselm?

Anselm was born in the valley of Aosta, then in the kingdom of Burgundy, in 1033; his parents, Gundulf and Ermenberga, were minor nobility, his mother devout, his father less so.[1] He had a sister, Richenza,[2] who married a man called Burgundarius, giving Anselm a nephew also called Anselm, who became a monk at Chiusa and died as abbot of Bury St Edmunds. At first Anselm had thought of becoming a monk in Aosta, then in 1056, after his mother's death and a quarrel with his father, he left home and never returned. He travelled north, into a country filled with the new excitement of both courtly love and the new theology of the schools. Nothing is known about this part of his life, but it seems he lived north of the Alps for the next three years. Entranced by learning, Anselm became a pupil of the great grammarian and scholar Lanfranc, then a monk and teacher at the new abbey of Bec in Normandy. Anselm finally decided to combine his love of learning with his desire for God by becoming a monk there himself in 1059. He became prior in 1063 and then abbot in 1078; he wrote and taught there for thirty-four years. In 1093, after the death of Lanfranc as Archbishop of Canterbury, Anselm was called to England to succeed him. He remained at Canterbury, except for two periods when he went into exile after quarrels with two kings, until his death in 1109.

Foremost among medieval philosophers and theologians, Anselm's works have continued to be read. His major theological work, *Why God Became Man*, was a discussion of the

1

theology of redemption, written while in exile in 1097 in Italy, and with this he made a summary of his argument in the form of a prayer, the third of his *Meditations*. He wrote two treatises on the existence of God, the *Monologion* and the more famous *Proslogion* which contains the well-known and much discussed 'ontological argument' for the existence of God. This was further supported by the *Reply to Gaunilo*. Other philosophical treatises were *On Grammar, On Truth, On Free Will*. As well as *Why God Became Man*, he wrote on other theological subjects: *On the Fall of the Devil, On the Incarnation of the Word, On the Virginal Conception and Original Sin, On the Procession of the Holy Spirit*. In addition he also composed a collection of *Prayers and Meditations* and a large number of letters. Some fragments of his spoken comments which were remembered and recorded also exist in a volume called the *Memorials of St Anselm*.[3] When he died at Canterbury aged seventy-six on the Wednesday in Holy Week 1109, he was still eager, on his deathbed, to explore new concepts and make them clear to others: almost his last words concerned 'a question about the origin of the soul which I am turning over in my mind . . . I do not know whether any one will solve it when I am dead.'[4]

It is 900 years since that moment of the death of Anselm at Canterbury; it was witnessed by a crowd of friends present at his deathbed and recorded by Eadmer, his secretary and biographer.[5] Anselm's works have been continually discussed since then, as a thinker who is always relevant. But in honour of this nine hundredth anniversary it seems appropriate to discuss not the only the thought of Anselm and his career in the arena of politics in church and state but his place among the saints, in his life and after his death, especially in the light of his understanding of heaven. Anselm's concept of heaven and the saints was a central theme throughout his life from childhood to death and it is possible to see why this was so, partly through Eadmer's account of him but mainly through his writings, especially his letters and his prayers and meditations.

Moreover, Anselm, both before and after his death, was himself regarded as a saint, and this can be highlighted by giving an account of his relationships with others on earth, as well as his overriding interest in establishing friendship with the saints in heaven.

This study of Anselm is different, not in material but in approach, from other accounts of his life and works. Perhaps every writer sees Anselm through his own interests and no doubt that is what I have done here. I have looked at Anselm of Canterbury in a different light from that in which he is seen by philosophers, theologians and historians. To philosophers, his works are still of positive intellectual interest; for theologians, his ideas about redemption are still relevant, if disputed; for historians, he occupies a major place in the history of England at the beginning of the twelfth century. Opinions of his writings and his life have not always been either favourable or consistent with one another. For instance, Bishop William Stubbs, the father of history in Oxford, saw Anselm of Canterbury primarily as a statesman, a reforming prelate who was yet a king's man whenever possible, loyal, but also a liberator who would strike a blow for the freedom of the English Church.[6] Again, an Oxford man, Richard Meux Benson, saw Anselm as the first of the wicked scholastics, the man who corrupted theology by dividing it from prayer: 'it seems to me', he wrote,

> that S. Anselm has done more harm than almost any teacher by his endeavour to make plain the Atonement and all other divine truths to the necessities of human reasoning; with the intention of making good this or that aspect of divine truth, he has first of all eliminated the divine life.

There were some who valued him as a man of prayer and used the *Prayers and Meditations* as Anselm wanted them to be used: for instance, Thomas Becket had a copy of the *Prayers* and used them often and with tears. Bishop Lancelot Andrewes knew the prayers of Anselm and included sections as an integral part of his great compilation for prayer, the *Preces Privates*, while one of the great men of the Oxford Movement, Dr Pusey, looked with seriousness at Anselm's works including the *Prayers* and made them available to the newly emerging Oxford Movement, though he thought of him primarily as an emotional medievalist, and spoke of 'the fervid language of this devotional writer', in his foreword to his translation of *The Prayers and Meditations of S. Anselm*, a translation in which out of the 18 meditations and 25 prayers, only two prayers and two and a half meditations are the genuine works of Anselm.[7] Anselm has been both praised and admired and also criticized for his actions and his writings, an approach which is equally true of the sparse discussion of his relics that concludes this study, where comments have been even more ambivalent.

These approaches to Anselm often reflected the concerns of the writers rather than those of Anselm himself. However, it seems to me that the increase in Anselmian studies since the days of Stubbs, Pusey and Benson has been considerable, and warrants a revision of their estimate. Anselm as a philosopher is perennially new and always discussed. On the political side a new look has appeared in a dialogue between Sir Richard Southern and Dr Sally Vaughn. Anselm's letters and his prayers are now considered as a serious part of his writings. All this I respect and accept. I have concerned myself, however, with what might be termed the celestial Anselm, his relationship with heaven, which was a focus central to his own life. In so doing I hope I have transcended rather than contradicted Bishop Stubbs who was, after all, one of the few Anglican bishops to approve of the restoration of religious life in the Church of England; I hope I have roundly contradicted Fr Benson, even though his community founded the religious community to which I belong; and I join Dr Pusey in admiration for Anselm, but by discerning, in the genuine *Prayers*, the genuine Anselm, not an emotional devotee.[8] Finally, after looking at the life of Anselm through his letters, his prayers, and the comments of others who knew him, to see how his theology shaped his lifestyle and relationships, in the later chapters of this book I have explored the history of his relics, his bones, his body.

I believe that the study of the small body of Anselm's genuine devotional works which is now possible can give a new picture of his place in Christian spirituality and theology; I think that many of the comments about him, adverse or otherwise, as a devotional writer, have been in fact comments on his imitators, not on his genuine works. I also believe that if he can at all be called the father of scholasticism with its consequent division of devotion and theology, it is *malgré lui*, and that what a true reading of the *Proslogion* shows is in fact a deep unity in Anselm between prayer and life and thought.

All Anselm's works survived and there are many manuscripts of them still extant. These have been given modern critical editions and most of them are available in translation. The basis for modern study of Anselm was the definition of the canon of his genuine works at the beginning of the twentieth century; the next stage was the edition of an established text. In the Middle Ages Anselm's writings were lost to sight under a host of spurious additions, a confusion perpetuated by the Maurist edition of Dom Gabriel Gerberon in 1675, and by Migne in his use of Gerberon's text for the *Patrologia Latina* in 1883. It was only in 1923 that this state of confusion was either observed or dealt with. Then, Dom André Wilmart began his systematic work of distinguishing the genuine works from the spurious additions, and he presented his conclusions in a series of articles between 1923 and 1932. These studies formed a foundation for the next stage, the edition of a text. Dom François Schmitt undertook the edition of the *Opera Omnia* which appeared in six volumes between 1938 and 1961; this work has been completed by the edition in 1969 of the *Memorials of S. Anselm* by Schmitt and Southern, the minor and less well authenticated Anselm; as the introduction to that work says, 'incomplete Anselm, or Anselm as others heard or thought they heard him'.[9]

Equally important for a true estimate of Anselm is the edition of a critical text of Eadmer's *Life of St Anselm* by Richard Southern in 1962; important for the light it throws on Anselm himself, but also for underlining the care with which his biographer recorded the circumstances in which most of Anselm's works were produced. There is also an account of Anselm as an international statesman and churchman in Eadmer's *History of Recent Events* and this can be supplemented by the comments on him in the Latin historians of his time. There is now a picture of Anselm which is not likely to be much altered by new discoveries, but which still needs to be drawn out in detail and applied. This is especially true with respect to Anselm as a devotional writer in the *Prayers and Meditations*, since they were the part of his works which suffered most severely first from the flattery of lesser imitators and then from the neglect of both Reformers and the Enlightenment.

Because of the stature of Anselm as a writer it seems proper to comment briefly on the links between his theology and his devotional works. The supreme example of this interplay between the prayers and the treatises is the third meditation, *On Human Redemption*, which is a summary, in the form of a prayer, of *Why God Became Man*. Here, the arguments about the manner of the atonement became a demonstration of the redeeming act of God in Christ, a personal encounter with what had been defined: 'Consider the strength of your salvation, and where it is found; meditate upon it, delight in the contemplation of it, taste the goodness of your redeemer, be on fire with love for your redeemer.' The intimate absorbing of what he understood about the atonement ('taste' is the word he uses, elsewhere, 'chew, suck, bite, swallow') led Anselm directly into prayers of adoration, of repentance, of thanksgiving and of petition, followed by a prayer of commitment to Christ: 'Draw me to you, Lord, in the fullness of love. I am wholly yours by creation; make me all yours, too, in love.'[10]

6

Another example of the link between thought and prayer in Anselm can be seen even more clearly in the realm of philosophy. The *Proslogion*[11] has attracted attention continuously, despite a period of neglect immediately after Anselm's death. Changes in modern understanding cannot be attributed to a new text, but change there has certainly been, especially in the 1930s. The *Proslogion* has challenged the interest of Thomas Aquinas, Descartes, Leibniz, Kant, Russell, Hegel and Karl Barth, and is still a lively matter for discussion. It would seem that it takes giants to misunderstand a giant. I will venture a few comments on the *Proslogion*, taking courage from Richard Southern's observation that a share of philosophical naivety is an aid to understanding Anselm's thought. There seems to have been general consent until this century to regard the *Proslogion* as containing a 'proof' of the existence of God, being in fact, the argument went, a series of logical propositions whose conclusion equalled 'God'. In 1931, however, Karl Barth discussed the *Proslogion* argument as being theological, not rationalist; he called it not an argument for, but a demonstration of, the existence of God. Two years later, Dom Stolz went further and called the *Proslogion* a mystical affirmation of a personal experience of God. Both these views were challenged by Etienne Gilson, who preferred the older approach of rationalism, but Barth's thesis stands, and forms an important stage in reinterpreting the *Proslogion*, and therefore queries Anselm's relation to scholasticism in general. This reinterpretation owes something naturally to the philosophical standpoint of Barth himself as a Protestant existentialist, but both he and Stolz formed their conclusions about Anselm from reading the *Proslogion* as a whole, and seeing it in the form in which it was written, as a prayer, rather than concentrating on isolated parts of books 2, 3 and 4 only. The phrase, 'faith seeking understanding', which Anselm coined to describe the *Proslogion*, is applicable to all his works and indeed encapsulates his entire approach to reality;

for Anselm, what was 'real' was not what was tangible but what was infinite.

The corpus of Anselm's works is established and available. It is a relatively small body of material, and because of the care with which Anselm wrote and published, the manuscript tradition is not difficult to interpret. Each treatise is complete in itself, but interrelated to Anselm's other works; he did not forget what he had written already, and start out on unrelated lines; he wrote with care and knew just what he wanted to say, what he wanted preserved, and in what order. Dom Wilmart has examined the recensions of one of his *Prayers to St Mary* which happen to have survived, and these show the extreme, meticulous care which Anselm took over words, phrases and the exact shape of the whole.

Anselm's life has been recorded in his own works, and that is the best place to get to know him, but also he lived at an era prolific in accounts of saints. He was the subject of two works by his contemporary, Eadmer, the *Life of St Anselm* and the *History of Recent Events*. These works were based on the observations of someone who had lived in Anselm's company for some years and who was an acute observer and careful writer. Such comments from observers are vital in understanding the past: as in the Gospels, in the *Lives of the Desert Fathers*, in the material relating to various saints but especially St Francis of Assisi, the saints are not known or loved primarily by their own written works. Many, including Jesus Christ, did not write at all, but they can be encountered through the human eyes and ears of those who knew them. Anselm is known still in what he wrote but this has to be complemented by these other sources.

Here Eadmer is the primary source. Eadmer was an English monk at Canterbury who became Anselm's friend and disciple. He was born about 1060, just before the Norman Conquest; of English background, he was brought up in Canterbury and absorbed there a love for English tradition which was modified only in a minor way by the influence of the European Anselm. He travelled with Anselm and kept a careful account of what he saw and heard. He claimed to have written his account from hearing it in Anselm's own words in conversation, and he said that he had shown his account to Anselm and gained his approval.[12] This was meant to give credibility to his work and has allowed the *Life* to be used, together with descriptions of Anselm's public life in the *History of Recent Events*, as a template for accounts of Anselm. However, Eadmer's interests and mentality were not always those of Anselm: Eadmer was a man of his times, with a love for the marvellous, for relics, for objects rather than ideas. For instance, at the Council of Bari, while Anselm debated the subtleties of the place of the Holy Spirit in the Trinity, Eadmer described a magnificent cope which had been made in Canterbury.[13] His *Life of St Anselm* is a remarkable book, since it is an early attempt to combine the two literary genres of hagiography and biography; it is a hagiography (*hagios*, holy) in so far as it parallels Anselm's life with that of the only model of holiness for a Christian, that of Christ; it is nearer to biography (*bios*, life), in that he claims to give an intimate view of Anselm in his earthly behaviour and contacts. Another source available for knowledge of Anselm is the canonization account by John of Salisbury, as well as references by historians such as William of Malmesbury. Anselm was well known and respected as a major writer in his own time, and also as a person of great goodness. William of Malmesbury, who had seen Anselm once and made a collection of his writings, said 'he was superior in wisdom and piety to all the men we have seen'.[14]

What can now be said about Anselm and sanctity in his life and writings? Many things, but I have attempted only three, and those in a brief and superficial way: first, I have examined Anselm's friendships on earth, then looked at his love of and friendship with the saints in heaven as it is reflected in his authentic works, especially in the *Prayers*; then, I have examined his own attitude to the relics of the saints and their veneration in his own experience; and I have concluded by assessing Anselm's cult in accounts of his burial, his canonization and his relics.

2

Anselm, friend of sinners: the penitent's desire for heaven

Anselm was loved as a good friend, and as a good man, but not as a man who was relentlessly good all his life. Many disagreed with him, especially in the political field, where his unparalleled clarity of intellect was a hindrance rather than a help in the compromise worlds of state and of church. He was opposed and criticized but many spoke of him as *sanctus* during his life, and Eadmer saw him as already among the saints. But this was by no means his own view of himself. There was in Anselm a quality of genuineness, a kind of basic self-knowledge, that kept him free from illusions and pretentiousness, and those who knew him recognized this. In the *Vita*, Eadmer says he learnt much about Anselm's early life from Anselm himself. 'He used', he says, 'as if in jest to relate in homely language in the midst of his other conversation what he did as a boy, as a young man, or before he adopted the monastic habit.'[1] It seems probable that these stories included the account Eadmer gives of Anselm's choice of a monastic way of life, which was by no means the edifying story one would expect, and says much for Anselm's lack of both pride and illusion that he repeated it, as well as for Eadmer's honesty that he recorded it. Apparently, in brief, he chose to join the small, new abbey of Bec in Normandy, rather than the greater and older foundation at Cluny, so that he would have more time for study; and he had nearly declined Bec also, for fear of playing second fiddle to Lanfranc. This was scarcely the immediate zeal for God which is usual in hagiography, if not in life.[2] The more he explored in thought the concept of God, the more he knew himself to be 'a poor little man' (*homunculus*), in need of mercy; this sense of his own humanity made him accessible to others, where his mighty scholarship could have been alienating.

One thing most vividly revealed in his personal *Prayers and Meditations* is Anselm's sense of his own sinfulness. These long and complex prayers for the inner chamber were offered for the use of others but there is no doubt that they were prayed as they were composed; these were no mere literary exercises, they were Anselm's real understanding of himself. They were deeply personal prayers, in the first person singular, and they contained all the exclamations and groans of the man who prayed them: 'vae, vae, vae hinc et vae illinc, – o miserrima et plus quam miserrima commutatio, heu, et heu . . . parce, deus, parce . . .'.[3] In spirit if not in fact the *Prayers and Meditations* can be compared to the manuscript pages of the *Preces Privatae* of Bishop Lancelot Andrewes which, says Drake, 'were happy in the glorious deformity thereof, being slubbered with his pious hands and watered with his penitential tears'.[4]

This emphasis on sin and repentance forms the first part of each of the prayers and meditations, and brings to life Anselm's more austere and technical comments about sin elsewhere. Sin for Anselm was not a personal psychological apprehension of wrongdoing and guilt: it was a theological truth about man in relation to God. 'Were it not better', he wrote in *Cur Deus Homo*, 'that the whole world and whatever exists except God, should perish and be reduced to nothing, than that you should do anything however small against the will of God?'[5] and elsewhere, 'how can any sin be called small when it is an offence against God?'[6] In the *Prayers and Meditations* this took on a passionate and personal intensity: 'I am afraid of my life. For when I examine myself carefully, it seems to me that my whole life is either sinful or sterile.'[7]

[God] is Most Just, and I have greatly sinned;
how should he hear my cry?[8]

O immoderate offence, offence against God,
how my sins cry out against me.[9]

Such self-abasement may seem overdone, but this was no self-conscious display of guilt for particular sins; it was rather the personal expression of Anselm's theological conviction about the state of humankind, including himself, and his first step towards changing this was to acknowledge and express its truth.

The first and second meditations contain lamentations for sin which are perhaps more intense than any of the prayers, though surely nothing can exceed the completeness of this, from the *Prayer to St Nicholas*:

I am buried in one abyss after another.
Woe upon woe; fear upon fear; sorrow upon sorrow.[10]

The earliest of the prayers, the second meditation, to which Anselm gave the subtitle, 'A lament for virginity unhappily lost', is entirely a lament for sin, containing only a final half sentence of hope. It is the most artificial in style of the prayers, and one that sounds to the modern reader to be verging on the hysterical. Dr Pusey said of it rather austerely, 'sin is continually in holy scripture spoken of as adultery against God and so it is here',[11] a comment perhaps more typical of Dr Pusey than revealing about Anselm. It seems to me that there is no reason for not taking Anselm to mean in this prayer exactly what he says: 'My soul . . . it is of your own free will that you are miserably cast down from the highest virginity to the lowest pit of fornication.'[12] On the other hand, and in spite of a phrase inserted by the editor in my translation of the prayers, about 'the wild youth' of Anselm, I think this 'loss of virginity' need not conjure up scenes of a sort of Rake's Progress through

Normandy into the cloisters of Bec. With Anselm's sensitivity to sin, his definition of 'adultery' was probably of the less picturesque kind.

The first meditation described the same sense of theological sin deeply felt: '*terret me vita mea,*' he begins, 'I am afraid of my life. For when I examine myself carefully, it seems to me that my whole life is either sinful or sterile.'[13] This sense of failure and loss was expressed in language which worked towards a crisis in a description of judgement, couched in phrases from the prophet Zephaniah which were to become familiar later in the crashing phrases of the *Dies Irae*:[14] 'The great day of the LORD is near, it is near, and hasteth greatly . . . a day of wrath, a day of trouble and distress' (Zeph. 1.14–16). This sensitivity to his own sinfulness formed the first part of each of Anselm's prayers; he used it as a tool for breaking through complacency into sorrow by the use of the basic emotion of fear, but it was more than a theological position.

A concern for the more external manifestations of sins emerged in Anselm's sermons and decrees against sexual infidelity and also in some of his letters, namely those to the youngest daughter of King Harold, the Anglo-Saxon princess Gunhilda, who had taken refuge in the abbey of Wilton after the Norman conquest. In the two letters Anselm wrote to her, he expressed clearly the kind of deeply felt yet entirely spiritual affection he had for others: he called her 'My beloved . . . my sister . . . my daughter according to the Spirit . . . my friend in God', and urged her to return to the monastic life: 'The charity by which I wish all men to be saved, requires me to love you with fraternal and paternal affection and to show solicitude for the salvation of your soul because of that love.'[15] Anselm was convinced that Gunhilda had been dedicated as a nun before she left Wilton in order to marry Count Alan Rufus, the greatest of the Norman barons in the north of England. For Anselm her first calling had priority: 'It is impossible for you to be saved in any way unless you return to the habit and vowed life which you rejected.' Count Alan Rufus died before their marriage and his brother (Count Alan Niger) inherited both his estates and Gunhilda; the brother also died, and at that point Anselm wrote another passionate letter urging Gunhilda to go back to monastic life:

> My sister, you have been ensnared; by this snare Christ is drawing you from one side but from the other the devil. By this snare Christ will either draw you to the heights of paradise if you hold on to the life of a nun, or – God forbid! – the devil will draw you into the depths of hell if you abandon it.[16]

There was in the same convent the princess Mathilda, a daughter of King Malcolm of Scotland. Count Alan Rufus, who eloped with Gunhilda, had been betrothed to the younger girl. Both had been living some form of monastic life at Wilton and, though both claimed that they had not made any religious promises, they could have been seen by some as committed to religious life. In the case of Gunhilda, this was the position Anselm maintained, seeing her salvation as intimately bound up with her return to the convent after two unproductive affairs. Likewise later he urged Mathilda to stay in the convent, which he certainly thought the more certain way to salvation, when she seemed likely to leave it for a new and even more prestigious political marriage to the King of England, Henry I. Anselm referred to her as 'a fallen daughter' whom 'the devil has caused to cast off the veil of religion'.[17] So far her situation had much in common with that which Anselm condemned in Gunhilda, but it was King Henry I who planned to marry her, and Anselm at last agreed that this was permitted, accepting that she had never made vows as a nun. He not only approved this royal marriage and blessed the pair,[18] he maintained close contact with Mathilda in person and by correspondence, and this continued with terms on both sides tender and gentle, in spite of the later quarrel between Anselm and Henry. Anselm addressed her as 'reverend lady, dearest daughter', and called himself 'your faithful servant, desiring your good in the present life and in the life to come'. She wrote to express concern for Anselm's physical health, and to assure him of her continued love and dependence, 'by whose blessing I was sanctified in legitimate matrimony, by whose consecration I was raised to the dignity of earthly royalty, by whose prayers I shall be crowned'.[19] It might sound as if Anselm had been persuaded by political expedience in both cases, but in fact with both women he was alert only to what he considered would secure their eternal happiness in heaven.

Anselm was rigorous in judgement but only for the end of salvation which he saw as the fullness of love. He was towards others as he was towards himself. His awareness of sin, and his sense of judgement, began with himself; it was overwhelming and yet the crisis of fear and guilt turned over, like the crest of a wave, into the other side of Anselm's prayer: 'But it is he himself, he himself is Jesus. The same is my judge, between whose hands I tremble', followed by a prayer around the name of Jesus, meaning 'saviour'.[20] From that safety, Anselm passed into the enjoyment of mercy; with his sense of sin he had an equal capacity for delight in receiving mercy. As in his life so in his prayer, he was able to enjoy as well as deplore; at the other end of the scale in the *Prayers* there was joy. Heaven and the joy of being with God forms the conclusion of each prayer: 'Let me be filled with your love, rich in your affection, completely held in your care'; 'I shall rejoice in you for ever to your glory'; 'In that perfection of charity of countless blessed angels and men, where no one loves another any less than he loves himself, they will all rejoice for each other as they do for themselves'; 'They will rejoice with their whole heart, and mind, and soul, so that their whole heart, mind, and soul will not suffice for the fullness of their joy.'[21]

And what lay between the hell of self and the heaven of shared love? Desire, a longing for God through Christ, what Jeremy Taylor later called 'a following after the most holy Jesus, in the contemplation of his life and death and resurrection'.[22] This personal involvement with the details of the sorrows and sufferings of Christ was a natural way for Anselm to pray. He understood the sufferings of Christ as the cost of redemption and expressed this theological conviction in the careful phrases of *Why God Became Man*; but it is in the *Meditation on Human Redemption*, the prayed version of the longer treatise, that this theory is made into a personal confrontation: 'Lord, you gave yourself up to death that I might live.'[23] This personal involvement with the kenotic Christ in the details of his sufferings was meant to provoke compunction, the piercing of the heart which leads from sin to salvation in the classic tradition of Christian prayer. It was an emotional involvement instead of an effort of the will, providing a setting for a traditional pattern and one which deeply influenced the whole of medieval devotion. It marked the same tradition in devotion that is seen in art by the change from the austere and crowned Christ on the cross in triumph to the human and suffering figure of the man of sorrows.[24] *The Prayer to Christ* was the one which most clearly reflected the emotions of the new devotion, but in it Christ was not seen in isolation. Beside Christ on the cross, Anselm pictured 'the most pure virgin, his mother'; and there was 'happy Joseph' taking down the Lord from the cross; and the angels of the resurrection, with their message, 'Fear not, Jesus who was crucified, whom you are seeking, is not here; he is risen'.

Most of the prayers asked the help of individual saints in order to pray to Christ – John the Baptist, Peter and Paul, Stephen, John the Evangelist, as well as St Mary and, less predictably, Nicholas of Bari, lately of Myra. The need for an intercessor, a friend at court who will speak a word with the great Lord, was behind this approach to prayer, and this also is closely linked with Anselm's more sober expressions of theology. Redemption was necessary, in Anselm's view of theology, but it was never simply an individual affair and it was never easy.

Mercy and justice had to be combined, and the image of a great king surrounded by courtiers who can ask him favours was one way of demonstrating the connection. The later medieval tendency in popular religion to attribute mercy to the Mother of God and leave justice to her Son is a corruption of Anselm's thought, certainly, but it could be derived from a reading of, for instance, the great court scene in the second *Prayer to St Mary*: 'The accused flees from the Just God to the good mother of the merciful God . . . good mother, reconcile your son to your servant.'[25]

In the *Prayers*, then, Anselm can be seen as he saw himself, sinful, alone, far from God, a sinner among sinners, before his Redeemer needing mercy and desiring with all his heart to belong to God in the companionship of heaven. He would do anything he could to attain this end, and he was also ready to enjoy the end when he has got it; he was no worried neurotic who would insist on feeling guilty and unworthy even in heaven, but one who was able to receive joy as a gift. Eadmer says a servant of his dreamt about Anselm after his death and heard him saying: 'There I live, where I see, rejoice and enjoy.'[26]

Anselm prayed his prayers in private but he was ready to share his meditations with his friends: in these highly personal prayers he communicated a whole method of praying which had that immense effect on medieval devotion that Sir Richard Southern called 'the Anselmian revolution.'[27] Anselm's life and prayer were one, and it was perhaps just because these prayers were really prayed out of genuine and deep need that they had the appeal they did. The prayers were verbal constructs, but they were not artificial: Anselm found himself to be in need of God, he experienced lethargy, the sense of alienation and dullness, before he wrote about it. His first premise in this way of prayer was that humankind is alienated from God and is therefore indifferent to him. In order to return, a person must want to respond and be prepared to try, by finding time, for one thing, and space to be still. Then apathy had to be broken through, and Anselm used every means by words and images to do this. From his own experience of compunction, that piercing of the heart by sorrow for sin, came his desire for God and his longing for heaven; and again words and images expressed and deepened this desire, which, according to Eadmer, was characteristic of his whole life – 'his whole desire was fixed on those things only which are of God'.[28]

Anselm has been described by David Knowles as 'a very great human being'.[29] This is a dimension of any person which is of interest; how rare it is to discover this in the lives of the saints is fully known only to those who study medieval hagiography and/or listen to the reading of the saints' lives in a monastic refectory. Without going so far as to apply the unfamiliar technique of psycho-history to Anselm, it is still possible to say something about the man himself as he appeared to his close friends in the *Vita S. Anselmi* and in records of his conversations.

Who were his friends? He seems to have enjoyed the small group of monks who shared his interests: Lanfranc, the monks at Bec and at Canterbury, Gundolf, Eadmer, Baldwin, Eustace, Alexander, Gilbert Crispin, Hugh of Cluny.[30] He once made a joking comparison,

> saying with cheerful good humour, 'Just as a owl is glad when she is in her hole with her chicks, and (in her own fashion) all is well with her, . . . so it is with me; when I am with you all is well with me, and this is the joy and consolation of my life.'[31]

Since his chief recreation was in such companionship, when he was deprived of it he was 'greatly afflicted'. In exile, in the hill-village of Liberi, his chosen retreat, Anselm was again always ready for both the solitude of prayer and the communication of friendship:

> he made himself 'all things to all men' (1 Cor. ix:22) helping everyone to the extent of his power, admitting to his conversation

all who wished to hear him without regard to who they were and satisfied each one with his kindness and affability whatever the nature of the subject they raised might be.[32]

What most impressed his contemporaries seems to have been his readiness to communicate with all who became in this way his 'friends'. With his stature as a scholar, one would expect the first impression to be of his erudition, and indeed the reputation he had in his lifetime for scholarship was great; Eadmer says of him,

> being continually given up to God and to spiritual exercises, he attained such a height of divine speculation that he was able by God's help to see into and unravel many most obscure and previously insoluble questions about the divinity of God and about our faith and to prove by plain arguments that what he said was firm and catholic faith.[33]

Obviously a great man for ideas, but not for obscurities; very often when one reads a commentary on Anselm's works, especially if it is by a philosopher, the impression one has is that if the commentary is so obscure, Anselm himself must be totally unintelligible. But Eadmer says the contrary: Anselm 'unravelled', not 'ravelled' many obscure questions, an observation which might lead readers to prefer a close personal look at Anselm himself instead of his commentators. He knew a great deal, but what impressed Eadmer was his willingness and ability to comunicate it. Anselm was available, he could be approached, he was a good companion – monks and clergymen enjoyed his conversation, but so did court ladies like the Queen Mathilda, and the rough tough Norman nobles of England, up to and including Earl Hugh of Chester, and it says a lot for Anselm's capacity for tolerance that he should have numbered him among his spiritual sons. The great monk, the ascetic, the scholar – all these were part of Anselm, but at the same time he was loved as a friend, as a good companion, as, simply, a good man. At table, abstemious himself, Eadmer says,

'If he saw any of them enjoying their food, he would give them a friendly and cheerful look, and full of pleasure, would raise his right hand a little, blessing them and saying "may it do you good."'[34] Moreover, though always eating sparingly, he could ask for something rather special and he knew he would enjoy it: when ill, he asked for partridge.[35] Anselm had more than one circle of friends: he had his monastic brothers at Bec and at Canterbury, and through correspondence he was in touch with a wider circle of those whom he knew as personal friends, scholars of like mind. As well as his rhetorical, passionate but entirely theological expressions of friendship, notable in his early letters, he expressed love for 'all men' but his realism caused him to acknowledge that he liked some people more than others. These were those whom he referred to in his *Prayer for Friends*:

> I pray for your mercy upon all men,
> yet there are many whom I hold more dear
> since your love has impressed them upon my heart
> with a closer and more intimate love.[36]

He enjoyed being with a small circle of intimate friends but he was at home also in the courts of kings and of popes and even, according to Eadmer, made a strong impression on Saracen soldiers employed by Count Roger during the siege of Capua in 1098:

> He [Anselm] was loved by all as a mild and gentle man, to whom in his own eyes no-one owed anything . . . the humanity of Anselm received all without any acceptance of persons, even pagans, not to speak of Christians . . . he was held in such veneration among them that when we passed through their camp . . . a huge crowd of them would call down blessings upon his head, then kissing their hands as they are wont, they would do him reverence on bended knees, giving thanks for his kindness and liberality.[37]

This capacity for love, for relationship, for caring for others appeared in the way the collection of *Prayers and Meditations* first circulated: they are intimate, personal prayers, revealing the writer, and making him vulnerable to those who read them. Yet he was ready to send such prayers to those who asked for them, and to give some advice about their use. He was not concerned about himself, his reputation as a writer or as a scholar: he simply wanted the recipient to use the prayers so that he or she would grow in the love of God, as he did himself. It is a supreme gift of friendship to share spiritual experience in this way, not as a teacher and spiritual master, but as a companion in the ways of tribulation and glory.

Anselm's awareness of sin in himself appeared in his sternness towards sin in others. In this he was not judgemental about people; rather it was a part of his care for them that made him offer the justice as the other side of love. He wanted everyone, and especially those whom he knew, to have the best of all gifts, the mercy of God, and he tried in every way to help them towards this end. For instance, as prior of Bec, he befriended the young, brilliant but wayward monk Osbern,[38] always 'encouraging him to improve'. His love for Osbern was expressed in a care which included discipline as well as gentleness:

> When he saw that he could rely on the firmness of the young man's good intent, he began to cut away all childish behaviour in him, and if he found in him anything worthy of blame he punished him severely.

At his unexpected early death, Anselm stayed at his bedside, serving him, through his last illness: 'he loved his son more than you could believe possible'; 'happy the youth to have such a friend!' At his funeral Anselm, 'weeping', went apart and eventually fell asleep; he dreamed that Osbern came and spoke to him about his present state. He then said mass every day for a year for Osbern and wrote several letters asking for prayers for his friend, 'who was happy and blessed in finding such love and such aid'.[39]

In his prayers Anselm included one for his friends and typically a parallel one for his enemies. Anselm's understanding of friendship seems to be all of a piece with his approach to other matters – friendship is defined not by personal attraction and liking so much as by relationship seen as reflecting the image of charity which is God. The letters which Anselm wrote at Bec as a young man were letters of friendship – in the majority, his chief aim was to express affection and friendship. But it was a union of wills in the service of God that he expressed with such passion and fervour, not personal liking or sentimentality. As in the *Proslogion*, it was the perfect friendship of heaven that was the pattern, 'that holy society where there will be unfailing and perfect friendship'. With monks he was constantly loving, but also severe, from a position of fraternal care. In a letter to a young monk, Lanzo, of Cluny, his austere advice was presented as from one poor monk to another:

> If anybody undertakes a monastic profession, it is good that he should concentrate all his attention on becoming rooted with the roots of love in whatever monastery he has made his profession. . . . Let him not pass judgement on the habits of others or the customs of the place, however useless they seem. . . . Let him put away every thought of migrating and rejoice to find himself in a place where he intends to spend his whole life, not unwillingly but of his own free will. And thus let him quietly give himself up to the diligent performance of the exercises of a holy life.[40]

Anselm's *Prayer to St Benedict* was filled with this sense of the monk especially as one under judgement:

> I profess to lead a life
> of continual turning to God
> as I promised in taking the name and habit of a monk;
> but my long life cries out against me
> and my conscience convicts me,
> as a liar to God, to angels, and to men.

Anselm had no criticism to make of the monastic way of life; it was not a human institution but a way pleasing 'to God, to angels, and to men'. He had promised to follow a way of life and be changed by it; therefore what he lamented was not that he was a monk, but that he was not a better monk. 'How dare I call myself a soldier of Christ and a disciple of St Benedict?'[41] he asked, and then pleaded with St Benedict to help him make better use of the rule and customs which, in turn, will cleanse him from sin; in fact, in order to be a monk, he must be a monk.

It is enough to mention the third meditation to show that in Anselm there was no divorce between theology and prayer, between faith and understanding, thought and life. But the real test case for this point of view is the *Proslogion*. Here Anselm proved himself to be pre-eminently a monastic and Christian scholar, using his mind to its limit in the search for God which is prayer. It would be wrong to ignore the structure of the *Proslogion* or to suppose the prayers it contains are mere pious appendages to an otherwise sensible work. It was written out of friendship, to help others, and it has the same basis as the prayers: the sense of sin and alienation to be overcome by desire for God. Anselm says himself that he wrote it in order to share his own joy in discovering this demonstration of what he believed about God; and he wrote it 'from the point of view of someone trying to raise his mind to the contemplation of God and seeking to understand what he believes'. It is faith in search of understanding, not a series of logical propositions which issue in a previously unknown conclusion. 'God is that than which nothing greater can be thought' is the basis from which his whole writing proceeded, not the end term of its arguments. Using credal, scriptural and dogmatic texts, as well as secular and rational concepts, Anselm expressed something that he, as a creature of God, had apprehended about his maker; and the very apprehension of this was a confrontation with God, since it was true, which further drew the one who believed into deeper understanding and belief.

This way of understanding the *Proslogion* is obviously far from the ordinary modern way of thinking, in which we believe that a statement is the end product of our thoughts and no more. Anselm's concept of truth and reality is involved here, and it seems that for him truth was an objective reality – in the treatise *On Truth*, he suggested two levels of truth: something which exists in the mind has a certain reality; if it corresponds to what is outside the mind, it has quite a different kind of reality; in the *Monologion*, he added that both these realities subsist in the highest degree of reality which is the mind of God. The *Proslogion* argument showed simply that God exists in intellect and reality, and cannot be thought to exist in any other way, which is unique. In both the atonement theology of *Why God Became Man* and here in the *Proslogion*, Anselm was not concerned to 'prove' anything, in a modern sense. He knew beforehand that, in the one case, God has redeemed humankind by the death of Christ on the cross, and on the other, that God exists and that certain statements are possible about him. He simply set out to show what it means to make such statements, and by the effort to understand, to assimilate what was already known. He was treating the docrine of atonement and the *Proslogion* argument as Eastern Christians treat an icon, as a way through, a way to be in touch with the reality that it represents in order to be changed by it. Here Anselm's thought had much in common with his understanding of monastic life and monastic ideas, and his view of personal relationships. It is a reminder that it was the objective routine of corporate daily liturgical prayer in mass and office which formed him almost unconsciously, as someone who received with others in order to understand. It was no accident that the ontological argument was revealed to him during matins.[42] The *Proslogion* is a prayer throughout, a prayer of desire and longing, in the best monastic tradition of longing. It ends with the great picture of the friendships of heaven already quoted. Anselm's understanding of friendship seems to have been all of a piece with his approach to other matters – friendship is defined not by personal attraction and liking so much as by relationship seen as reflecting the image of charity which is in God. The letters which Anselm wrote at Bec as a young man were letters of friendship, but it is a union of wills in the service of God that he expressed with such passion and fervour, far more than personal liking and choice. As in the *Proslogion*, it was the perfect friendship of heaven that was the pattern, 'that holy society where there will be unfailing and perfect friendship'.

These prayers were Anselm's own dialogue with Christ and the saints; but they also formed another part of his friendships on earth in their use and dissemination: when asked to do so, he would send copies of his prayers which he had written down, to others, together with suggestions about their use. In a preface he set out advice for their use which in many ways was innovative:

> The purpose of the prayers and meditations that follow is to stir up the mind of the reader to the love or fear of God, or to self-examination. They are not to be read in a turmoil, but quietly, not skimmed or hurried through, but taken a little at a time, with deep and thoughtful meditation.
>
> The reader should not trouble about reading the whole of any of them, but only as much as, by God's help, he finds useful in stirring up his spirit to pray, or as much as he likes. Nor is it necessary for him always to begin at the beginning, but wherever he pleases.
>
> With this in mind the sections are divided into paragraphs, so that the reader can begin and leave off wherever he chooses; in this way he will not get bored with too much material but will be able to ponder more deeply those things that make him want to pray.[43]

The prayers were an intimate gift, not a straitjacket: they were offered for quiet reading, not the whole at once, but only what was useful to the individual, what he would choose, what pleased him and would make him want to pray. This way of prayer was to be centred on the individual praying, and to be shaped by his changing needs. It was to be undertaken alone and in solitude, 'in the inner chamber' both of the place and of the self, where the only companions would be the company of heaven, those closer to Christ. The basis for this was 'fear of God' and 'self-examination'. These prayers were intimately filled with Anselm's own self-knowledge and repentance, as well as with thankfulness and praise of God; they expressed his lifelong desire for God, his sense that he had to stir up the mind, stir up the spirit, in order to come fully alive in discipleship. The basic human emotions of love and fear, based on self-examination, were to be used to the full to stir the one praying out of apathy and sloth into fullness of life. This is the pattern that was worked out in every prayer and meditation.

The prayers were available for all, not just for monks. The basis of sorrow for sin applied equally to monks and laypeople, self-knowledge was where everyone began. Anselm was asked about prayer and heaven by two laymen sent to him by Hugh the Hermit. In a letter to him, Anselm said he wished 'to inspire the minds of secular people to love the eternal kingdom'.[44] This care of a hermit for laypeople also caused Anselm to write a most affectionate letter about prayer to another layperson, this time the lady Frodelinda, a friend of Hugh the Hermit.[45] His prayers were also sent with letters to both the princess Adelaide and Mathilda of Tuscany. The fact that he had such a non-monastic audience points to the conclusion that though Anselm remained sure that monastic life was still the safest way to God, it was clearly not the only way. The life of heaven with the saints could be realized upon earth by everyone: 'give love and receive the kingdom' was for all. This was part of the long tradition of the consultation of hermits by laypeople, from the deserts of Egypt in the fourth century through to Europe into the fourteenth. The advice given by Anselm to Hugh the Hermit to help the laymen who had approached him for guidance was not about conduct or morals or theology but about how the gift of the love which is God could be received and allowed to shape life. Given that centre, everything else followed naturally: as Antony the Great put it, 'All God wants is the human heart.'[46]

3

Anselm, friend of the saints

———•◦•———

Eadmer considered Anselm in his daily life to be a saint and in his accounts of Anselm he constantly shaped his words to convey the likeness of Anselm to Christ. This does not mean that Eadmer made up events, only that he gave them the hue of sanctity. After all, Eadmer was a companion of Anselm for many years, and others were with them who saw the same events. Sometimes the interpretation of Eadmer differed from Anselm's own view, and from the view of others, but the events themselves were not in question. For instance, when Anselm went onto exile in 1097 he travelled with members of his household, notably two monks from his own abbey of Bec, Eadmer and Baldwin. Unfavourable winds prevented the party from sailing from Dover. Anselm, impatient to be on his way to Rome, said,

> 'If it be the will of God that I should return to my former miseries rather than get free of them and pursue that purpose on which he knows I have set my mind, let him see to it and so dispose; I am ready to obey his will. For I am not mine but his.' . . . 'Tears stood in his eyes, while our hearts were smitten with sorrow at what we saw and heard.'[1]

A change of wind took the ship on its way and Eadmer's description was written to imply that this was in answer to Anselm's submission to the will of God. The event is not in question nor Anselm's tears, but Eadmer's account of it was deliberately given with echoes of Gethsemani and Christ's 'not

29

my will but thine be done' (Matt. 27.39). It was not Anselm who saw a wonder of answered prayer – he simply prayed with tears, typically, that he might be patient under the hand of God, in adverse circumstances; it was Eadmer who implied that his prayer was heard and answered through an external event.

The crossing to Wissant was observed by Eadmer and also by Baldwin, another member of Anselm's household, an experienced monk who had come to Canterbury from Bec to take charge of the practical side of affairs. More credulous or perhaps less subtle than Eadmer, he noticed a miracle about the crossing which he related to Eadmer many years later: 'In the bottom of the boat which had carried the archbishop over the waves, a plank had been broken making a hole almost two feet across . . . but no water had entered while Anselm was aboard.'[2] Baldwin told Eadmer that he and the owners of the boat, who had pointed out the damage to him, considered this a miracle but he had not let anyone publicize it at that time. Later he insisted to Eadmer that this was a miracle of preservation by God, a parallel to Eadmer's account of the change of wind. It was not a story Eadmer could ignore so he included it, but simply as Baldwin's story, without shaping it into his narrative. In both cases, the companions of Anselm saw something happen; one of them looked for an external wonder, the other saw significance, while Anselm followed his own way of repentance and submission through prayer in dialogue with God.

In using Eadmer's accounts of Anselm it is important to see what he was doing as a writer. Neither the *Life* nor the *History* are straightforward historical pieces of writing though it is proper to see plain events and relationships within them. It is clear that Anselm was seen in his own lifetime as a man of prayer and also a man of warmth and kindliness. He was with friends when he went into exile, and Eadmer recorded the enthusiastic welcome he had from others as he travelled: he was welcomed everywhere by 'monks, clergy and people'[3] and eventually by the Pope.[4] But from his style of writing, it is also clear that Eadmer saw Anselm as always in the company not only of earthly friends but linked into the dimension of heaven: 'With what anxious care, with what fear, with what hope and love he addressed himself to God and his saints.'[5] He was not noted as a dramatic self-confident thaumaturge like Bernard of Clairvaux,[6] but simply someone who was already on good terms with heaven.

In Anselm's own writings, especially in his prayers, it is possible to see how the love of companionship with others which characterized his life was applied naturally by him to the saints, as those who were already with Christ. This was true from a very early age. In an account which he himself gave to his companions at Canterbury of a dream in his childhood this theme of a company of saints as friends was already present:

> Now Anselm, their son, when he was a small boy lent a ready ear to his mother's conversation, so far as his age allowed. And hearing that there is one God in heaven who rules all things and comprehends all things, he, being a boy bred among mountains, imagined that heaven rested on the mountains, that the court of God was there, and that the approach to it was through the mountains. When he had turned this over often in his mind, it happened one night that he saw a vision, in which he was bidden to climb to the top of the mountain and hasten to the court of the great king, God. But then, before he began to climb, he saw in the plain through which he was approaching the foot of the mountain, women, serfs of the king, who were reaping the com, but doing so carelessly and idly. The boy was grieved and indignant at their laziness, and resolved to accuse them before their lord the king. Then he climbed the mountain and came to the royal court, where he found God alone with his steward. For, as he imagined, since it was autumn he had sent his household to collect the harvest. The boy entered and was summoned by the Lord. He approached and sat at his feet. The Lord asked him in a pleasant and friendly way, who he was, where he came from and what he wanted. He replied to the question as best he could. Then, at God's command, the whitest

of bread was brought him by the steward, and he refreshed himself with it in God's presence.

The next day therefore, when he recalled to his mind's eye all that he had seen, like a simple and innocent boy he believed that he had been in heaven and that he had been fed with the bread of God, and he asserted as much to others in public.[7]

These words are close to the pattern for prayer which emerged later in Anselm's life. The themes of desire, repentance, self-knowledge and companionship were all there. The child wanted to reach God who, he believed, lived at the top of the snow-capped mountain which loomed over Aosta; the man desired always to 'ascend' to God and wrote at the end of the *Proslogion*:

My God,
I pray that I may so know and love you
that I may rejoice in you.
And if I may not do so fully in this life,
let me go steadily on
to the day when I come to that fullness.[8]

The child saw others being idle instead of working, in a state of uncaring 'torpor', which became one of the mature Anselm's favourite words for the inner idleness of soul which prevents prayer; the child wanted to see others rebuked: the man saw his own 'torpor' and rebuked himself. The child entered into dialogue with God, replying to questions about who he was, where he came from and what he wanted: the man posed the same questions to himself, notably in his prayer to John the Baptist ('Alas, what have I made of myself').[9] Moreover, the child was not alone with God on the mountain; he saw there another servant of God (*dapifer*) with him and God: in the same way, for the man, the spiritual presence of others, friends in heaven as well as those on earth, was fundamental. He was a sinner with men, a saint with saints. Moreover, as the child declared publicly the details of his dream, so the man was ready to share the intimacy of his prayer with others. The child received 'the whitest of bread': Anselm wrote a prayer to be said before communion which continued to be his best-known work and at the end of his life, 'he wished to be present at the consecration of the Lord's body which he venerated with a special devotion and love'.[10] He had always received the sacrament in church with others, 'in order to be incorporated into your Body "which is the church"'.[11]

This sense of fellowship within the Body of Christ was not contradicted by his concern for solitude:

Come now, little man, . . .
Enter the inner chamber of your soul,
Shut out everything except God.[12]

It was to a solitary, the hermit Hugh, that later he wrote a letter encapsulating the unity he saw between solitude and companionship with the saints:

Dearest brother, God proclaims that he has the kingdom of heaven up for sale. For the kingdom of heaven is such that neither the eye of mortal man can see nor his ear hear nor his heart imagine its blessedness and glory. So that you may be able to imagine it I say this: if anyone deserves to reign there, whatever he wills shall be done in heaven and on earth; whatever he does not will shall be done neither in heaven nor on earth. For so great shall be the love between all those who shall be there and between themselves, that they shall all love each other as they love themselves but all shall love God more than themselves. . . .

Those who fill their hearts with love of God and their neighbor will nothing but what God wills or another person wills – as long as this is not contrary to God. From this it follows that they press on eagerly by prayers, conversations, and meditations on heavenly things, because it is pleasant for them to desire God and to speak and hear and meditate about him whom they love so much. From this it follows that they rejoice with those who rejoice, weep with those who weep, mourn with those who mourn and give to the needy: because they love others as much as themselves.

From this it follows that they despise riches, power and pleasure and being honored and praised. For someone who loves these things often does something contrary to God and his neighbor. For on these two commandments depend all the law and the prophets. Give love, therefore, and receive the kingdom; love and possess.[13]

He then referred the recipient to his similar description of the fulfilment of all relationships in the *Proslogion* as his own understanding of heaven. It was the same pattern as the dream of the child: desire, an ascent, dialogue and self-knowledge, communication to others, before the ultimate rest with others in the presence of God.

Anselm lived 'surrounded by a great cloud of witnesses' (Heb. 12.1). This sense of dialogue with the saints in heaven necessitated solitude, withdrawal and stillness; it is notable that the theme of hermit life was present to Anselm also as a young man when he was trying to decided on his future career: 'I want to dwell in a hermitage',[14] a reflection perhaps of the renewed interest in hermit life in the west in this period exemplified by the hermit orders such as Camaldolese and the Carthusians, as well as by growing numbers of individual hermits.[15] This need to be alone and withdrawn was not a contradiction to Anselm's love of company; earlier ages, unlike our own, were capable of holding several ideas in their minds at once without hypocrisy or tension. Anselm, began the *Proslogion* with this need for withdrawal:

> Come now, little man, . . .
> Enter the inner chamber of your soul,
> shut out everything except God
> and that which can help you in seeking him. . . .
> Now, my whole heart, say to God,
> 'I seek your face,
> Lord, it is your face I seek.'[16]

But he ended it with a vision of total fulfilment in heaven, whatever had been longed for on earth, there would be given in abundance – beauty, speed, strength, health, drink, food, music, pleasure, wisdom, power, riches, security, unity, but above all, friendship: 'If it is friendship that delights you, they will love God more than themselves, and each other as themselves.'[17]

'Loved by all' for his human kindness and availability, Anselm seemed to Eadmer, who based his expression of his insight into Anselm on many passages from the Gospels, especially the Beatitudes, to walk the earth as a saint among men. He was 'at home' with all men, but he was equally at home in the courts of heaven. There, the saints were his friends, and in his prayers he addressed them as such. They were more fully alive to him than his earthly friends; they were the great ones already alive in Christ *in patria* who had achieved friendship with the King of kings to which Anselm also desired to be admitted; they were accessible to those still on earth to give help and encouragement to those *in via*. People, living and dead, formed together the body of Christ, and Anselm understood communion with both.

Anselm can be seen as connected with the saints in two ways: first through his prayers, second, himself a recognized saint after his death. In the first approach, his prayers to the saints are comprehensible if one understands the context of meditation based on Scripture, before seeing how in the field of meditation, his influence was inestimable. Since the barbarian invasions, prayer in the Latin west had been based on the Latin Bible, the sacred Scriptures, heard, read or seen. It had formed the imagery through which reality was explored, both as a pantechnicon containing all knowledge and as that to which all learning was to be brought for its elucidation, but above all as a word of God to the soul. It was copied often and gloriously, and studied closely, so that the commentaries upon the 'Sacred Page' were integral to it. It was read aloud and presented in preaching and teaching, illustrated in the decoration of churches, known by heart through the liturgy. The Old and the New Testaments were read as one single book by one author, God, who spoke to his people in the time of the Law and in the time of Grace, illuminating both for the reader by the person of Christ. A comment by Origen (c.183–c.254) on the text of Genesis summarizes the medieval approach to Scripture:

> If anyone wants to hear and understand this according to the literal sense, he should listen to the Jews rather than the Christians. But if he wants to be a Christian and a disciple of Paul, let him hear what is said according to 'the law of the Spirit,' and let him consider what is said . . . in an allegorical sense. We are given such allegories, but it is not easy for anyone to discover all their meaning, so we must pray from our hearts that the 'veil might be taken away'. If anyone wants to be converted to the Lord, 'for the Lord is Spirit', let him pray from his heart that the veil of the letter might be taken away and the light of the Spirit come, as it is said, 'we all with open face behold as if in a glass the glory of the Lord and are changed into that image from glory to glory as by the Lord the Spirit.'[18]

This theme of glory communicated through the word of the Scriptures to the believing heart provided the basis for prayer and devotion; according to Claudius of Turin (c.830): 'Blessed are the eyes that see divine Spirit through the letter's veil.'[19]

The Bible was not known alone; the concept of sacred Scripture was extended in some ways to the commentaries of the Fathers of the Church, which were mined by preachers and pastors as well as forming the basis for meditation. This knowledge of the text through symbolic, spiritual, commentary affected devotion at every level, usually linking the text with doctrine about Christ or/and interpreting it in relation to the hearer. For instance, in his commentary on Genesis, Bede (673–735) interprets a passage of the Old Testament thus:

'Four kings with five ... took Lot the son of Abraham's brother ... when Abraham learned that his kinsman Lot had been taken captive ... he went in pursuit ... and brought back his kinsman' (Genesis 14.9, 12, 14, 16). Here we see Abraham as the mystical figure of Christ who by his passion and death redeemed the world from death in battle against the devil.[20]

There is here interest in words of the Bible as illustrating redemption in Christ for the hearer now, not in the possible meaning of this text in its original context. The medium through which the glory of the Lord and the light of the sacred page were received was for most Christians not so much through reading written words but through hearing them said or sung, most of all through the poem of the liturgy, with the glory of buildings and ritual reflecting for the eyes the wonder of praise. Attention was concentrated on what was prayed and seen to be prayed in church, so that the church became an antechamber of heaven. Along with eucharistic celebration went the ordered public prayer of the Divine Office where the continual public reading, at fixed hours of the day and night, of the prayer book of the Bible, the Psalms, offered a vehicle for the expression of praise and repentance, as their christological sense was drawn out by context and form. This sense of glory and the wonder of what God has done in Christ was reflected in the gold of the crosses and the richness of other church ornaments, in the beauty of language, of music, stained glass and painting. The buildings contained sacred space in which even the stones cried out in praise, though again and again preachers affirmed that external glory was only of value to God if matched by inner conversion. In a sermon for the anniversary of the dedication of the church at Jarrow, Bede added, after commenting on the external glory of church building and ornaments both in the Temple of Solomon and in his own monastery:

The marvellous workmanship that went into the construction of the Lord's earthly house [has delighted] you as you heard about it and so . . . these details spiritually understood [should] arouse our minds to more ardent love of our heavenly dwelling place.[21]

This sense of the immediate presence of the kingdom of God was linked to a view of history which pervaded both speculation and action. Time, which had begun with the expulsion of Adam from paradise, was, with the coming of the new Adam, Christ, in its final phase; this was the sixth and last age of the world, in which glory was constantly breaking through from the majority of Christians already in heaven to those still on earth. The contact of Christians in this world with the saints was no wistful sentimentality but a practical awareness of their united life in Christ: the saints lived in the 'seventh age' of the world which was thought to run concurrently with the sixth, present, age from the birth of Christ until the end of the world; both would find their culmination in the eighth and last 'age', the day of the Lord.[22] It was the theology of redemption that was being expressed and offered, assimilated and prayed.

The words of the Scriptures provided the basis for meditation, but there were other prayers written down, some in the form of collects, and who knows how many were said privately, based on the Scriptures; most of all it was the Psalter, the basis of the daily office of the monks.[23] That formed the basis for Anselm's devotion and in effect that was the background to his whole life as a monk, as well as the basis of his prayers and meditations. In fact his own contribution to communicating the work of meditation began there: he was asked to provide 'flowers from the psalms' (a common custom) to help in meditation, but to these he quickly added meditations in quite another vein:

Herewith the 'Flowers from the Psalms' which . . . you deigned to command me to choose for you. . . . After the 'Flowers from the Psalms' I have added seven prayers . . . give them your whole attention and do it as well as you are able, so that with humility of mind and the feeling of fear and love the sacrifice of praise may be offered.[24]

What difference did Anselm's prayers make to this tradition of compunction through biblical meditation? They provided new and personal material for prayer and they were also a definitive personal link between the saints already in the presence of God and those praying on earth. The saints with whom he primarily claimed friendship were those he found in the Bible, especially those mentioned in the New Testament as closest to Jesus Christ during his life or, in the case of Paul, well acquainted with the disciples soon after the crucifixion. They all had their place already in the calendar of feasts of the saints in the annual cycle of office and mass, and already there were brief personal prayers to them.[25] The first heavenly friends for Anselm were Mary, Peter, Paul, John the Baptist, John the Evangelist, Mary Magdalene, Stephen; to these he added two later saints, Nicolas and Benedict, for different reasons. But above all these he claimed his closest bond of love to be with Jesus Christ. The only pattern for Christian sanctity, in fact as well as in writing, is of course the life and death of Jesus Christ, and for Anselm Jesus was pre-eminently his way to God. In his *Meditation 1*, he wrote this passionate section about the name of Jesus, foreshadowing the cult of the name of Jesus which was later given further impulse by Bernard of Clairvaux:

> Jesus, Jesus, for your name's sake, deal with me according to your name. Jesus, Jesus . . . Dear name, name of delight, name of comfort to the sinner, name of blessed hope. For what is Jesus except to say Saviour? So, Jesus, for your own sake, be to me Jesus. . . . O most desired Jesus, admit me to the number of your elect, so that with them I may enjoy you, with them I may praise you, and glorify you with 'all those who love your name,' who with the Father and the Holy Spirit shall be glorified for ever.[26]

Here Anselm invoked the name of Jesus in its root meaning of 'saviour' and described Jesus as dear, full of delight, comfort and hope; but however personal, this was not exclusive; the union with Jesus was not a mystical flight of the alone to the alone, but a prayer to be part of the body of Christ which is composed of all who are in Christ, and therefore a part of the dynamic community which is the Trinity. In his prayer to Christ, likewise, it is the person of Jesus dying on the cross which was Anselm's desire and love: here Jesus was addressed in even more passionate terms – Anselm wished he could have been present at the crucifixion, not alone but in company with Mary and with Joseph of Aramathea:

> Alas for me that I was not able to see
> the Lord of Angels humbled to converse with men. . . .
> Why did you not share
> the sufferings of the most pure virgin,
> his worthy mother and your gentle lady? . . .
> Would that I with happy Joseph
> might have taken down my Lord from the cross. . . .
> Would that with the blessed band of women
> I might have trembled at the vision of angels.[27]

The compunction of heart that Anselm sought was entirely personal but not isolated; his companionship with Jesus was part of the return of all humanity to God. In each prayer, in fact, Anselm directed his words to Jesus as the way to God, and asked for the mercy of Jesus Christ and his continual help and friendship, along with the prayers of the saint whose help he was soliciting, in order to become someone able to receive such mercy more and more completely.

After Christ and only because of him, Anselm claimed the Mother of Jesus, Mary, as his friend and heavenly patron. The three prayers to St Mary, especially the third prayer, illuminate not only Anselm's doctrine of the Mother of God, which he does not specifically elaborate elsewhere, but throw light upon his whole theory of the incarnation, lighting up and making real the dry sentences of the treatises *On the Incarnation* and *Why God Became Man*. This was a period when an increasingly human and humane love of Mary was flourishing, alongside an increasing devotion to the humanity of Jesus, and this was reflected in the prayers. Alongside this was the new romanticism of chivalry and the vocabulary of *adoratio* for a lady and this also had its parallels in Anselm's prayers to St Mary, 'lady' and 'queen'. Anselm took great care over his prayers to St Mary. He had been asked for such prayers by a brother at Bec, and also by Gundolf monk of Bec, Bishop of Rochester and close friend of Anselm. Along with the prayers he sent him, Anselm addressed a letter in 1072 to 'Gundolf from Anselm who is Gundolf's Anselm':

> I composed one prayer as I was asked to do, but I was not satisfied, knowing what had been asked, so I started again and composed another. I was not satisfied with that either, so I have done a third which at last is all right.[28]

The manuscripts of the third prayer[29] show that Anselm continued to change it, giving a great amount of time to it. He was meticulous about his written work; by night he 'corrected mistakes in manuscripts'.[30] He was never more careful than in relation to the prayers he addressed to Mary. The three prayers were kept together and they followed his pattern for meditation: the first showing his need to wake up and pray; the second used the emotion of fear to reach repentance 'when the mind is filled with fear'; while the third 'seeks the love of Christ and Mary'. Here Mary was always addressed as primarily the Mother of Jesus Christ, born sinful like all humankind and therefore belonging to all humankind, so she can be called 'lady of the world', 'mother of the life of my soul', 'nurse of the redeemer of my flesh', 'mother of the creator and saviour'. She was not to Anselm in any way a bride, or a lover as in later devotion; he did not approve of the new doctrine of the immaculate conception of Mary, popularized by his nephew Anselm of Bury. It was her consent to bearing Jesus which made Mary the first of the redeemed, and therefore Anselm found no title too great for her: she was most holy, life-bearer, shrine of goodness and mercy, lady of might and mercy, most gentle, mother of God, human virgin, great beyond all measure, queen of angels.

> Oh beautiful to gaze upon,
> lovely to contemplate, delightful to love . . .
> at what a height do I behold the place of Mary,[31]

he exclaimed, but his claim to her friendship rested not upon any innate glory in herself but upon her childbearing of Jesus, her redeemer. On a more personal note, when he was in Capua, at night Anselm fell into a broken cistern, and he spontaneously turned to Mary and exclaimed 'Holy Mary!' (*'sancta maria'*) as the saint most concerned with his bodily well-being – one of his very few recorded exclamations.[32]

It was not only Jesus and Mary that Anselm loved as friends, but also others who had died and now lived in Christ. In his prayers, he spoke to them as both friends in the future and helpers here and now.

In his prayer to John the Baptist Anselm at once called him 'friend of God' who was

> so great a friend of God . . .
> To you . . . whom grace has made such a friend of God,
> to you, in my distress, I flee.[33]

John was addressed as the forerunner, the one who acknowledged the Lord before his birth at the meeting of Elizabeth and Mary; above all he was seen as the one who baptized Jesus and addressed him as the Lamb of God, the one 'who takes away the sin of the world'. Anselm presented himself to God therefore as most in need of this cleansing; he used the idea of the creation of humankind in the image of God, which he said he had defiled in himself, and therefore could claim the attention of the one who was the first to bring people to Christ, the restorer to the true likeness. There is here the long patristic tradition of image and likeness presented with passion and immediacy.

In his *Prayer to St Peter*, Anselm addressed him primarily by titles found in Scripture, as shepherd of the faithful (John 21.15) and as doorkeeper of the kingdom of heaven (Matt. 16.19). Anselm talked to this saint particularly casually, even taunting Peter with his betrayal of the Lord:

> He [i.e., Anselm himself] may have strayed but at least it is not he who has denied his Lord and Shepherd.[34]

For Anselm, St Paul was the apostle to the Gentiles, but most of all a 'nurse of the faithful',[35] one to whom the image of mother could be applied. Paul was a mother, like Christ, the mother and nurturer of Christians. In a long passage Anselm addressed both Paul and Christ as 'mothers' in their care for humanity, as well as 'fathers' in their severity. It was therefore in the character of a child that Anselm appealed for the help of Paul in his way towards God.

John the Evangelist Anselm called 'beloved of God', the 'friend of the heart', and he wrote two prayers to him 'to ask for the love of God and those near him'.[36] Here Anselm was insisting on the good offices of John as the most intimate of Christ's friends, who would understand an appeal to affection. John was addressed as the beloved disciple who leaned on the Lord's breast at the last supper and also as the evangelist and letter writer, with quotations from 1 John 3.17 and from the Gospel (13.25 and 19.26). This is an early instance of the use of the figure of John being singled out as the special friend of God, and as an example of personal affection. In the usual pattern of his prayers, it is both terror and shame, as well as the adoration and thankfulness that this rouses in Anselm, that leads him to shape the two prayers. Like John, he longs to be capable of loving God as he is loved by him but knows how far he is from this state; the beginning for him was to know this and then, with John, receive love as a gift.

The prayer to Mary Magdalene, as lover and as penitent, addressed her as the one who 'came with springing tears to the spring of mercy, Christ'.[37] The setting for the beginning of the prayer was Mary of Bethany's washing the Lord's feet with tears; in this Anselm accepts the liturgical conflation of several Marys in Scripture[38] into one figure of great love and great repentance, and therefore contemplation. Here she was addressed as 'the blessed friend of God', 'your beloved Mary', 'chosen because you are beloved and beloved because you are chosen', but Anselm also presented himself as a sinner alongside one who had been a notorious sinner, and in an almost teasing turn of phrase, as with Peter, he says to her:

> Recall in loving kindness what you used to be,
> how much you needed mercy,
> and seek for me that same forgiving love
> that you received when you were wanting it.[39]

Anselm placed himself alongside the saints by referring to their earthly life as sinners like himself, so that their interest in praying for him might be awakened as a friend and co-sinner. This prayer, like the prayer to Stephen, was sent to the princess Adelaide: for 'the increase of love' it was to be said slowly and 'from the depths of the heart'.[40] It is the most lyrical of all the prayers, and in it Anselm showed a sensitive concern for the emotions of Mary Magdalene. The setting of the second half of the prayer is the meeting of Mary Magdalene and Christ in the garden of the resurrection, and here Anselm examined each detail and explored particularly Mary's tears. He expanded the great dialogue 'Mary', 'Rabboni!' (John 20.16), paraphrasing Christ as saying:

> 'I know who you are and what you want;
> behold me;

do not weep, behold me;
I am he who you seek.'

Anselm commented:

At once the tears are changed;
I do not believe that they stopped at once,
but where once they were wrung
from a heart broken and self-tormenting
they flow now from a heart exulting.

In the prayer to Stephen the first martyr, Anselm begins with a stern description of his own and therefore of humanity's sinfulness. The second half is about the love which made Stephen pray for his enemies when they were stoning him to death. Since Stephen had shown such love towards his enemies, so that evil was turned to good, Anselm claimed his help to turn his own misery and loss into love and praise: 'holy Stephen, blessed Stephen' is also 'loving Stephen', and so he exclaimed:

I need someone to help me.
In love and assurance I seek you as my intercessor,
that you may make peace
between me and your powerful friend,
the Lord and Creator of both you and me.[41]

It is the story of Stephen's martyrdom in Acts that shapes Anselm's prayer; as always, he is using the Scriptures as a basis for personal involvement with God and the saints.

Two other saints Anselm addressed were non-biblical but in some way associated with him. For instance, there is a prayer to St Nicholas, who was supposed to have been the fourth-century bishop of Myra; he was venerated with special devotion in Anselm's monastery at Bec, as well as throughout the coastal areas of England and France, as the patron of sailors. It may have been the removal of his relics from Myra to the western port of Bari under the care of the Normans on 9 May 1087 (see pp. 70–1) that initially prompted Anselm to write this prayer.

In 1093 he wrote to Prior Baudry and the monks of Bec to ask for a copy of 'the prayer to St Nicholas which I composed'.[42] The prayer may have been rewritten, or simply included as it stood in collections of prayers sent to others. It begins with an extended lament by Anselm for his own sinfulness.

> He is Most High and I am weak;
> how can my voice reach up to him? . . .
> I will pray to one of the great friends of God.

'Why', he asks St Nicolas,

> are you called upon by all men in all the world
> unless you are to be the advocate of all who pray to you? . . .
> I do not ask you to defend me but to pray for me.[43]

There is a confidence in the saint as one who must care for sinners which Anselm puts forward for his own encouragement.

The *Prayer to St Benedict*, the seventh-century founder of monasticism in the West, whose rule was known and followed by Anselm all his adult life, was based on the words of the Rule rather than Scripture, as was the case in the other prayers. It is about true discipleship and true authority for any Christian. In both, Anselm was rigorous in presenting himself as, in himself, a failure. For instance, in the *Prayer to St Benedict* he wrote:

> I profess to lead a life
> of continual turning to God,
> as I promised by taking the name and habit of a monk;
> but my long life cries out against me
> and my conscience convicts me,
> as a liar to God, to angels, and to men.[44]

He urges Benedict to feel responsible for such a disciple and therefore to help him.

There is the same theme in his prayer to the saint of any church where he might be in charge as either abbot or bishop (and he was both at Bec and at Canterbury). He saw himself as entirely in the hands of God for the sake of others and wrote, with his usual teasing suggestion, that it was Christ and the saint who were to blame for his appointment and must therefore make good his deficiencies:

> You have made an ignorant doctor, a blind leader,
> an erring ruler.
> For you have done this,
> either by commanding it or by permitting it.
> So it is you . . . who must act – you by praying, and you by
>   giving –
> so that what you have done
> may hold back neither me nor others.[45]

He saw the congregation as his equals and friends, for whom he has been made responsible:

> Jesus, good shepherd, they are not mine but yours,
> for I am not mine but yours. . . .
> Let them not weigh upon me,
> but neither let me be a burden to them. . . .
> Let them not be held back by me, sir,
> by whom they ought to be led forward. . . .
> Carry me and them, excuse me and them!
> Help us all, rule and protect us all,
> so that I may rejoice in their salvation with me,
> and they in mine with them.[46]

In the *Prayer to St Benedict* all his fellow monks were seen as friends in equal need; and in the *Prayer by a Bishop or Abbot*, those committed to his care were also seen as friends who will pray for and with him. All the emphasis was on the mercy of God conveyed *to* him and *through* him.

Here Anselm was exploring the concept of the true exercise of authority as responsibility, echoing many earlier writers, notably Gregory the Great in *On Pastoral Care* and the sermon of Augustine of Hippo on the anniversary of his consecration as bishop:

For you I am the bishop; with you I am a Christian. 'Bishop' – this is the title of an office one has accepted to discharge; 'Christian' – this is the name of the grace one receives. How full of terror is the one, how full of grace is the other.[47]

Five other shorter prayers followed the same pattern though without involving the saints: the prayers for friends and for enemies, the prayer before Communion have already been discussed, and the prayers to God and to the Cross provide no new insight into Anselm's love of the saints. Those that relate to the present theme of Anselm among friends, dead and alive, are the prayers directed to asking the help of the saints.

In none of these prayers was Anselm's theology weakened by sentimentality; but his intellectual clarity of the mind was turned here into personal and impassioned prayer. He was of course well aware of the overwhelming love of God for his creatures and for those redeemed in Christ, and that this redemption was already accomplished on the cross. But Anselm was always equally well aware of his own lack of genuine response to that gift of salvation, and his prayers were all directed towards an increase in himself of the capacity to receive and transmit that love while on earth and so to be ready for its fullness in heaven. He stressed always that saints have had to pass the same way into redemption – none were born good. And so, as with his friends on earth, Anselm talked with the saints in heaven freely and with a certain assurance. There was a realism about Anselm, a lack of sentimentality, which marks him out from both those who looked for miracles in his life and other saintly figures who were his contemporaries. As with so much else, as will be seen, Anselm was both of his age and above and beyond it.

4

Anselm and the veneration of relics

———◆———

Anselm wanted to be a friend of the saints who were the friends of God and in this he reflected his own times; the desire for heaven and the sense of the companionship with the saints here and now as patrons, guardians and intercessors was basic to medieval religion at every level, of person, time and place. It was not difficult to see Anselm as eventually one among the saints. But in one respect Anselm was not typical of his times. This was in the cult of relics, which was to many another way of contacting the saints. In order to see how exceptional Anselm was in his attitude to relics it is necessary to comment on the growing cult of the saints at the places where their bones rested in this period.

The veneration of the bones of the holy dead was not a late development in Christian history, but something which was there from the first. All Christians were by Pauline definition 'saints' (Rom. 1.7) who by death entered more fully into the life of Christ, and all bodies of the Christian dead received respect and were buried with honour in the earth from which God had taken Adam, 'for as in Adam all die, even so in Christ shall all be made alive' (1 Cor. 15.22). But in public worship and in private devotion, the physical remains of certain Christians who had shown in life and in death special signs of the indwelling of Christ were held in unique respect and this developed into the cult of the saints. The promise of resurrection in Christ was for all, but certain Christians, because of external factors, became a special focus for this belief at their deaths. The fact that corporate, public expression of veneration focused on the bodies of some individuals was occasioned most of all by the public spectacle of steadfast faith to the point of death by those who suffered as martyrs in the sporadic persecutions which came to an official end in the Roman Empire with the peace of the Church in the early fourth century. Those who had known the martyr and supported him by their prayers, even watched his execution personally, did not collect souvenirs in order to remember atrocities: what they wanted was to retain a tangible link, through whatever remained of his earthly body, with the glory he had entered into with Christ. The aged Bishop of Smyrna, Polycarp (d. *c.* AD 157), wrote to the Philippian Christians of the chains of those arrested for their faith as 'the diadems of those who have been truly chosen by God and our Lord'[1] with a serenity which was notable also when he knew that he himself was to be taken to the arena and killed there: 'he was filled with a joyful courage; his countenance was filled with grace.'[2] Many who knew him had been present to the end:

> Thus at last, collecting the remains that were dearer to us than precious stones and finer than gold . . . in joy and gladness we will be allowed by the Lord to celebrate the anniversary of his martyrdom both as a memorial for those who have already fought the contest and for the training and preparation of those who will do so one day.[3]

There is no suggestion the martyr (a word meaning 'witness') was making any political statement by his death, nor did any Christian martyr harm others deliberately in the act of dying. Nor was pain in itself the focus of 'martyrdom'; the bones were not collected and preserved to commemorate suffering inflicted. Any pain endured was seen as 'precious' because it had been for the martyr a refining fire, a gateway opening into life while he was suffering, not just a reward added on afterwards. Like Stephen, the first martyr (Acts 7.59–60), these deaths were specific and public instances of the union with the death of Christ on the cross which was the pattern for death for all. The bones of such public figures were not simply buried and left alone; the place of burial became a natural focus for a yearly joyful commemoration of this birth into heaven.

The ritual commemoration of these deaths-into-life was the celebration at their graves of the Eucharist, the great thanksgiving for the passover of Christ through the cross. It is noteworthy that eucharistic images were naturally linked to martyrdom, as in the letters which Ignatius of Antioch (d. *c.* AD 108) wrote when on his way to his own death in Rome: 'I am God's wheat and I am ground by the teeth of wild beasts that I may be found pure bread of Christ.'[4]

For the early Church, the martyrs and the apostles (who were also martyrs) were the first rank of saints. However, the relatively informal and spontaneous response of a local community to its own martyrs changed in several ways, with the expansion of the Church, the increase of heresy, the distance in time from the events, all of which led to the need for a more formal examination of doctrine and life of those who had died in this way by those who had not known the persons concerned. Who were truly to be regarded as martyrs? It was not the lion that made the martyr, and perhaps some suffered death who might have held erroneous views. The leader of the local community, the bishop, was eventually held to be especially responsible for doctrine, and it was his duty to make sure that those whose names were inscribed in the list of martyrs commemorated by his church had been sound in faith and in conduct.

In the public corporate prayer offered by Christians in church the bones of the martyrs had a special role. The celebration of the Eucharist and the offering of prayers at the tombs of the martyrs is attested as early as the beginning of the second century. Their first burial places were in cemeteries outside the walls of cities, as can be seen at Rome, and at Canterbury. After the peace of the Church, the bones were brought into the basilicas in the cities, both in order to have them available and, later, for fear of barbarian attacks. They were placed under the altars, so that the mysteries were always celebrated in the presence of the saints, in the antechamber of heaven. It was a practice not without its critics: in the fourth century Vigilantius had criticized the practice and earned a scornful answer from Jerome:

> So you think then that the bishop of Rome does wrong then when over the dead men, Peter and Paul, venerable bones to us but to you a heap of common dust, he offers up sacrifices to the Lord, and their graves are held to be altars of Christ?[5]

The calendar of the Church included the death days of the martyrs and also the days of the translation of their relics, which was done with pomp and circumstance. The weekly calendar of festivals was expanded and embellished by the names of these friends of God. Special hymns, chants, prayers and sermons were offered for the saints on these days, and eventually the readings of the monks in choir included a third section which, after the Bible and the Fathers' commentaries on Scripture, prescribed for reading aloud either extracts from the writings of the saints or condensed accounts of their lives and deaths. Bishops were enthusiastic about their possession of the relics of saints and could be somewhat cautious about passing them on. Paulinus wrote to Severus:

> Our brother Victor has informed me that you, as is worthy of your faith and grace, want for the basilica which you have built the blessing of the sacred relics of the saints whereby your church should be adorned. The Lord is my witness that if I had even a scruple of sacred ashes more than I need for dedicating the basilica which will soon be completed in the name of the Lord, I would have sent it to you.[6]

The form of the church was constantly affected by the presence of the saints. Their bodies were buried near the altar, either under the altar, or over it, the coffin either forming a backdrop to the altar, or lying at its side. Later, the presence of crowds of pilgrims necessitated the creation of a crypt behind the main chapels and under the altar, if any dignity was to be preserved in the conduct of services in the main body of the church. Churches were deliberately built in the form of reliquaries, the coloured glass taking the place of jewels. Stars on the ceilings represented the saints in heaven, icons and frescoes on the walls attesting their continued presence in the liturgy. The bones themselves asserted the presence with believers of those who had already passed through death into life and were living in the seventh age, awaiting with them the eighth day of God in the very place where the Eucharist opened the gate into the heavens.

In the fifth century, the most venerated scholar of the Latin West, the aged Bishop of Hippo, Augustine, illustrated his theology of the resurrection by describing miracles connected with the arrival of the bones of St Stephen in his church. Public healings took place and were recorded by order of Augustine, eventually forming part of the twenty-second book of the *City of God*. In his sermon three days after Easter day, Augustine presented the evidence of a cure by the relics of St Stephen in the persons of a brother and sister from Caesarea, Paulus and Palladia:

> I made the brother and sister stand on the steps of the bishop's throne, just below the level from which I addressed the congregation, while the narrative was read. . . . Then indeed there arose such a clamour of wonder, such a continuous shouting, mingled with tears, that it seemed impossible that it should ever end. . . . What do these miracles attest but the faith which proclaims that Christ rose in the flesh and ascended into heaven with the flesh?[7]

The theological point that human flesh had been and could be the living temple of the redeeming power of Christ was made again and again. Given a theology of the creation of the whole person in the image of God, and using the anthropology of the times, there was no reason to think that the flesh was any less holy after death. Cyril of Jerusalem taught his catechumens that 'there reposes in that body a power greater than that of the soul itself, the grace of the Holy Spirit'.[8] The tombs and what they contained were gateways into heaven, and there the human remains of a fellow Christian could be touched and would in turn touch the present needs of the living in an unbroken and indeed reinforced bond of love. 'Think what things God reserves for us in the land of the living, he who bestows things so great from the dust of the dead.'[9]

Healing of sickness was part of a demonstration of power of God over the demons. Jerome relates how the Emperor Constantine translated the relics of Andrew, Luke and Timothy to Constantinople, 'before whose relics the demons howl',[10] and Ephraim the Syrian wrote of the living presence and power of the dead through their remains:

> See how the relics of the martyrs still breathe! Who can doubt of these martyrs being still alive? Who can believe that they have perished? For the deity dwells in the bones of the martyrs and by his power and presence miracles are wrought.[11]

Given such a focus for healing, the popularity of visits to the place of the burial of the saints was assured. At first, the bodies of the saints were kept severely intact, awaiting their resurrection whole, but the division of the remains of the saints ceased to be forbidden as the need for the holy bones became more widespread among the new churches. Places which had no martyrs wanted them and asked for parts of them: towards the end of the sixth century, for instance, Gregory, Bishop of Tours (*c*.540–94), related in his *Glory of the Martyrs* how his deacon 'received relics of some martyrs and confessors from Pope Pelagius of Rome' (d. 590), which he then identified as relics of the apostles and 'Paul, Laurence, Pancratius, Chrysanthus, the virgin Daria, John and his brother, the other Paul'.[12]

There was also a sense of the need for personal and individual contact with the saint in more tangible ways than corporate prayer. A fragment of bone or a fragment that had touched a fragment, even a speck of dust, could be taken and carried away for use in need and for affectionate meditation. Not only were churches eager to have these relics, but individuals also wanted to own them. Already in the second century, alongside the public veneration for martyrs such as Polycarp, Cyprian and Ignatius, their disciples personally kept rags dipped in their blood. Such personal relics might be kept at home, worn around the neck in a chrismatory, or on the hand in a relic ring, or simply carried in a pouch or pocket. Wilfrid of Hexham collected fragments of bone on his visits to Rome and when he was in Gaul, which he carefully labelled, and those he presented to various churches in Britain,[13] but he had also his own private collection in a chrismatory which could be worn round the neck. During his quarrel with Irmunberga, the wife of Ecfrith of Northumbria, Wilfrid was imprisoned and the queen 'took away the reliquary of the man of God which was filled with relics and (I tremble to say it) she wore it as an ornament both in her chamber at home and when riding about in her chariot'.[14] This was not done of course out of devotion, but as a taunt to Wilfrid.

Bishops were in a good position to collect relics when they travelled, but it was not only churchmen who had them. Emma the wife of Cnut secured the arm of St Bartholomew. Gregory of Tours owned a reliquary that had belonged to his father who had 'put the sacred ashes in a gold medallion, and carried it with him', relying on its help during a perilous journey. After his father's death, Gregory's mother wore the gold medallion round her neck, and later still Gregory himself carried the reliquary with him in his pocket.[15]

Such relics were not 'official'; they were meant never to be exchanged for goods or sold for money; for of course such private ownership was wide open to abuse. Carpetbaggers had entered into the removal of parts of saints' bodies with enthusiasm. A new category of *pia furta* – the good deed of theft[16] – indicated that it was better to steal a relic than to buy it. With individuals the matter was difficult to check, since the acquiring of a relic in itself was a private, almost secret, matter. Many would go to extremes for this privilege of an intimate tangible contact with a piece of heaven. Few wanted to know if relics really were what they claimed to be; what mattered was: did they work? And if they did, then they were what they claimed to be. Augustine of Hippo was eager to demonstrate the power of the relics of St Stephen (see p. 53), and so also was Bernard of Clairvaux: at the funeral of his friend, Malachy of Armagh, Bernard wanted to demonstrate the power of the dead body. There was a boy with a withered hand present and Bernard took him by the hand and, he said, 'I laid it on the bishop's hand and he brought it back to life. . . . Surely the grace of healing lived in the dead man.'[17] In both cases, the miraculous event guaranteed the sanctity of the bones, not vice versa.

Many of those who respected and used medieval relics were, like Augustine and Bernard, people of outstanding intellect, and they were not condescending to the simple when they knelt before the body of a saint; they were applying the same intelligence that caused them to produce the works that have never been equalled such as the *City of God* of Augustine of Hippo, or the *Sermons on the Song of Songs* of Bernard. Ways of thinking have changed, certainly, so that today intellectuals would rarely venerate relics, but that is not to say that present-day understanding of reality is closer to the truth than any system of the past; 'different' is not always 'better'.

By the eleventh century, the cult of relics was universally accepted and employed, with increasing emphasis on collections of fragments of bones made by individuals for themselves. Eadmer was interested in having a collection for himself and seems to have been unable to accept that Anselm did not share this concern. Anselm was in many ways a man of his own times, but in respect of the cult of relics he was an exception, though to think of him as taking a cool modern view of relics would be to misunderstand him. He was concerned about the canonization of saints and he respected their physical remains, even if he was no eager collector of such relics. In the collection of relics which Eadmer kept for him, there were two hairs of the Virgin, a fragment of St Neot and one of St Prisca. Anselm did not reject or criticize them, but seems to have ignored them, perhaps taking them for granted. Over the offer of one relic, Eadmer says Anselm 'rejoiced greatly', but he handed it to Eadmer to keep. He did his duty as requested about the relics of St Neot, but fragments went to Bec or to his chaplain; his mind was always concerned with what lay beyond physical objects, in this case, the realities of heavenly life.

He was, however, ready to apply his mind to questions about saints, their lives and their relics. For instance, in restructuring the liturgical life of Canterbury, Lanfranc, his predecessor as Archbishop, wanted to remove from the cathedral the relics of any saints which were not widely known and authenticated. He said to Anselm, 'These Englishmen among whom we are living have set up for themselves certain saints whom they revere but . . . I cannot help having doubts about the quality of their sanctity.'[18] In this Lanfranc reflected new questions being posed about canonization: what mattered was not only 'does this work here and now?' but was this miracle-working property the work of God as a confirmation of goodness of life or of true martyrdom? As Lanfranc put it, 'the quality of sanctity' now needed the support of records of virtues. There ensued a dialogue between himself and Anselm at Canterbury about this which was recorded by Eadmer. Anselm's comments show that his concern was always for the honour due to the 'friends of God' rather than legal, physical, philological or even national matters. Lanfranc told Anselm that he doubted the quality of the sanctity of English saints hitherto unknown to him, in particular Alphege. Alphege had been the Archbishop of

Canterbury who had been killed in London on 19 April 1012 by Viking invaders, and his body had been transferred to Canterbury in 1023. He was deeply revered by the English and many miracles were recorded at his tomb. Lanfranc suggested he was not a true martyr because he had not chosen to die rather than renounce Christ, but because he refused to buy himself off at the expense of others. Anselm, already more ready to respect the English saints than Lanfranc, replied to this legalistic quibble with an argument he was to develop later in *De Veritate*:

> What difference is there between dying for justice and dying for truth? ['*veritas et justitia*'] Christ is both truth and justice so he who dies for truth and justice dies for Christ. . . . It is not unfitting that that one who is truthfully pronounced to have suffered death voluntarily for so great a love of justice should be numbered among the martyrs.[19]

Lanfranc was convinced by this, and ordered the continued veneration of Alphege at his tomb in the cathedral, even adding to it by commissioning the monk Osbern to write a new account of Alphege and having it set to music.

Anselm's comments, recorded by the Anglo-Saxon Eadmer, may have been meant to suggest that Anselm had a regard both for the past of the English and for the relics of saints, as Eadmer did himself, but this was very far from the case. As in so many matters, Anselm was considering this purely as a theologian. Anselm saw Alphege's actions as those of a true martyr, and compared him to John the Baptist. In his prayer to John the Baptist he had seen John the Baptist, like Alphege, as a martyr although dying for truth rather than for Christ; he stressed the friendship of the martyr with God, and the gift of grace therefore given him by God, and it was in this category that he spoke about Alphege.

Anselm had learned respect for the Anglo-Saxon traditions of both monasticism and sanctity from the dissident monk

Osbern, who had been sent from Canterbury to Bec to be retrained by Anselm. Anselm returned him to Canterbury, having learned from him, as well as forming him as a scholar, recommending 'his fervour for prayer seasoned with a sense of joy and his progress in knowledge through perseverance in study, coolness in thinking, and a tenacious memory'.[20] These skills, honed by Anselm's care and encouragement out of unpromising material, were to make Osbern a pre-eminent writer and one who revered the English past, and that respect he communicated to Anselm.

Anselm, however, was not ready to respect any of the dead just because they were Anglo-Saxon or because their relics were the focus for miracles. He accepted that there were Anglo-Saxon saints such as Alphege but he was not ready to admit that Waltheof, executed for treason by William the Conqueror, was one of them. He was firm that no reverence should be paid at the tomb of Earl Waltheof, who had become a symbol to many of the English of their nation's past. Waltheof's tomb was at Crowland Abbey, which prompted the historian Ordericus Vitalis to write in his favour, and he also had a shrine at Romsey Abbey. In a letter to Stephen the Archdeacon of Winchester, Anselm ordered him to go to Romsey Abbey and tell them to 'completely forbid that any honour of the kind due to a saint be paid by them to that dead man whom certain people wish to have as a saint'.[21] In another letter to Abbess Athelits and the conclave of English nuns at the abbey of St Mary at Romsey, whom he addressed as 'dearest daughters', Anselm forbade veneration of Waltheof under threat of excommunication. He begins, however, with his customary statement that what he was doing was because he loved them and desired above all their salvation; for this reason they were to 'take away from the dead man from now on all honour of the kind due to a saint and do not make any offering to him'.[22] His intervention was in line with canon 26 of the Council of Westminister (1102) which had decreed that 'No-one without the sanction of the bishop is on his own responsibility to attach sanctity, as we have known it done, to the bodies of dead persons.'[23] The ambiguous situation about the cult of Waltheof came from the fact that in 1075 he had joined the revolt of the earls against William the Conqueror. However, he had repented, confessing his guilt first to Archbishop Lanfranc, and then in person to William, who was at the time in Normandy. He returned to England with William but was arrested, brought twice before the King's court and sentenced to death. He spent almost a year in confinement, where he was said to have spent the months of his captivity in prayer and fasting. He was beheaded on 31 May 1076 at St Giles's Hill, near Winchester, and his body was initially thrown in a ditch, but was later retrieved and was buried in the chapter house of Crowland Abbey. In 1092, after a fire in the chapter house, the abbot had Waltheof's body moved to a prominent place in the abbey church. When the coffin was opened, it was reported that the corpse was found to be intact with the severed head rejoined to the trunk. This was regarded as a miracle, and the abbey, which had a financial as well as a national interest in the matter, began to publicize it. As a result, pilgrims began to visit Waltheof's tomb as a shrine to a martyr, and after a few years healing miracles began to occur there. It seems that Romsey Abbey was also a focus for veneration of some part of the relics of Waltheof. He became a focus for Anglo-Saxon loyalty as well as the inhabitant of a miracle-working shrine. Unlike that of Alphege, Anselm did not consider his death to have been that of a martyr: he saw him as an Anglo-Saxon thane who had been rightly executed for treason by William the Conqueror. Anselm saw no evidence of the sanctity of martyrdom and therefore he concluded that his relics were not working true miracles; and also saw it as his responsibility as Archbishop to make a stern intervention; apparently the sisters at Romsey Abbey had initiated this by writing to ask his advice. Anselm was not objecting to the veneration of a saint's relics but asserting the evidence needed for such an action, in line indeed with the new papal decrees; the evidence of miracles at the shrine was to Anselm no longer the only proof of sanctity.

Another comment on the bones of another English saint is to be found in Anselm's letter to Bishop Robert Bloet of Lincoln. This was about Anselm's treatment of St Neot's relics when Anselm was Abbot of Bec:

> May you know for certain that I myself, when I was abbot of Bec, made investigations at St Neots (1080) and found in a box which they call a shrine the bones of the holy and treasured confessor Neot. I immediately replaced them in the same box except for one arm, which is said to be in Cornwall, and a small part, which I kept for myself as a memorial and in veneration of that saint. Having carefully shut up this box with the same bones inside, I took the key back with me to the church of Bec, where it is carefully preserved to this day. Let God reward each one in eternal life and let the saint intercede for them before God as he knows to be expedient for them.[24]

He then urged the bishop to give support to the construction of a church in honour of St Neot. A relic list at Bec includes 'St Neot'. Undoubtedly Anselm gave his own 'small fragment' into the eager hands of his chaplain. The community in Cornwall had been refounded as a house of Bec in Lincolnshire in 1134, and this was where Anselm had explored the casket of relics. This Cornish hermit was mentioned in Asser's *Life of Alfred* as a patron of Alfred[25] and this link was exploited in later *Lives* of St Neot. It was through the eleventh-century *Annals of St Neots* that the best-known story about Alfred – the burning cakes – came to be told. Anselm had no interest in Neot and his sanctity but, as he had been asked to do, dealt correctly with the relics. It was, however, 'eternal life' that he mentioned in his letter to Bec: 'Then let the saint intercede before God as he knows to be expedient for them.'

Anselm was always concerned with living friendship with the saints in heaven in relation to life here and now; he would answer questions about saints or examine relics if he was asked to do so, but he was not spontaneously interested in their relics. In this he was unlike other saintly bishops, of whom a notable later example was the Carthusian Hugh who was Bishop of Lincoln about a hundred years later. His biographer wrote:

> He had a ring made for his relics of the finest gold set with precious stones which had in the part which encircled the outside of his finger a kind of hollow jewel which he intended to use as a repository for relics. This receptacle was about the width of four fingers, and in it he had collected thirty relics of the saints.[26]

Hugh, although a member of the new hermit-order of the Carthusians, went to extreme lengths even by the standards of his own day to collect even more pieces of relics, gnawing two fragments of bone from the arm of St Mary Magdalene during a visit to Fecamp, 'first with his incisors and then with his molars'.[27] When venerating the arm of Oswald of Northumbria at Peterborough, he cut off a piece of a protruding sinew: 'this he kept and preserved with great devotion.'[28] He had also a personal golden casket of relics which he gave before his death to the Carthusians in Italy, while the ring was presented to the cathedral in Lincoln.[29] Archbishop Stephen Langton, likewise a zealous collector of bones, removed some of the bones of Becket for his own use when assisting at the translation of the martyr. Anselm, with all his reverence for the saints, was not, it seems, concerned with visiting or amassing their relics; it was Eadmer who followed the relic-collection track.

Relics which were associated with St Mary the Virgin were equally of little interest to Anselm, which is surprising considering his great devotion to her as saint in heaven. According to the New Testament, the person closest to Christ in his earthly life was his mother, Mary. All that is known of her life is written in the discreet pages of the Gospels and Acts; the romances of the *Protevangelion of St James* add nothing to what is known about Mary in the Gospels, which can be summed up in her phrase, 'Be it unto me according to thy word' (Luke 1.38). In her the greatest of miracles took place: God became man. As Augustine had said, there are three miracles: the virgin is a mother, the word becomes flesh, God is made man. Mary was entirely absorbed by her Son, and any other account of marvels in her life would seem impertinent.

This was not the case, however, with later thought about Mary. Both theological reflection and devout meditation were confident that one so near to Christ must share especially closely in his redeeming work, and moreover be compassionately ready to use her intimate place to plead for sinners. This way of reflecting attributed to her innumerable miracles after her death, made her the centre of the most important pilgrimages of the Middle Ages, and provided her with relics. The presence, however, of her relics is unexpected, since Mary, like her Son, was held to have been taken straight into heaven at her death. Like the Holy Sepulchre of Christ, the tomb in which the Virgin's dead body was laid was found to be empty. No body, no relics. No bones of the Virgin Mary have ever been invented but, even more than in the case of Christ, devout imagination demanded physical, tangible relics, most often of an intimate kind. Some are connected with the infancy of Christ, some with his death, and a few simply with Mary's person. Her shift, her slipper, her hair, drops of milk from her breast, provided the emotional focus for the building of great cathedrals, and drew pilgrims in thousands. With no warrant whatever in Scripture, the relics of the Virgin became an essential part of medieval life, and those connected with the passion of Christ were especially prized. The hairs of the Virgin came into this category. However, when some of 'the hairs of the Virgin' were offered to Anselm by Ilgar Bigod, a crusader, it was not Anselm but Eadmer who collected them up and gave a detailed account of them. His account runs as follows:

While Anselm was at Rouen there arrived there Bohemond, one of the most noted leaders of the Jerusalem campaign, who had in his company a cardinal of the church at Rome, named Bruno. This cardinal had a Master of the Knights named Ilgyrus, an active man, of no little repute among his fellows . . . He had been known to Anselm from his youth and had received many kindnesses from him. So, being on terms of friendship with Anselm, he entertained him with a great deal of agreeable talk of the wars he had been through. He also disclosed to him the fact that he was in possession of many relics of saints and the way in which he had come by them. Among these, and indeed above all of those he possessed, he prided himself especially on some hairs of Mary, the blessed Mother of God, of which he said that some had been given him by the Patriarch of Antioch when he held there the post of Master of the Knights under Bohemond. He added: 'I should not, I confess, have dared to take these hairs, had I not been moved to do so by love of this my native land where I was born and brought up. I hoped some day to come safely back here and with these relics to glorify my country. So now, as under God's protection I have not been disappointed in that hope, I have determined to give two of them to this Church which is the very centre of Christianity for the whole of Normandy, two to the Abbey of St Peter and St Auden, two to the monastery of that same Virgin of Virgins in which, under your care, I grew up to man's estate, and two to yourself. The Bishop of Antioch gave me twelve of them altogether, declaring that according to what, as he asserted, he found written in the records of ancient writings, which among them were held to be of great authority and were kept with the archives of the Church over which he presided, these hairs had been torn out by that Lady herself when, standing beside the cross of her Son, a sword pierced through her soul.

That is what he said, Anselm, filled with joy over these relics, after making with the Archbishop of Rouen and Bohemond and those back from Jerusalem the arrangements which seemed appropriate, returned to Bec. But, as the hairs of which Ilgyrus had spoken had been left at Chartres where Bohemond's family and most of his goods were awaiting his return, the Archbishop of Rouen and the Abbot of Bec sent some men of the monastic order to fetch them. This was done. And when those who were bearing the relics which Rouen was to have were approaching the city, the Archbishop, accompanied by the canons and all the clergy of the city, together with the monks of St Auden and an immense crowd of the whole population, went devoutly in a long procession to meet them and receiving them with all possible honour carried them into the church and deposited them there in the most sacred place. Four of the hairs were taken to Bec. Of these Anselm reserved two for Bec and the remainder reverently for himself; and as I was the Keeper of his Chapel and responsible for its arrangement, he delivered these to me to take care of, which I have done right up to the present day. What others feel about them I do not know; but for myself I know quite certainly that . . . father Anselm always regarded them with great reverence and that I myself by experience holy and sublime have felt that there is about them something great and a mark of holiness which should be embraced by the whole world. So much then about those relics.[30]

The story of the origin of the relics was told in this form to Anselm, but another historian had a different slant on the provenance of the same relics at their presentation in France:

During his sack of the city of Jerusalem (scouring the city and killing Saracens) Ilgar entered the holy sepulchre and he said that the native Christians who had remained in the church spoke secretly with him and, wishing to secure his protection, obligingly guided him and his companions and showed them certain things they and their ancestors had long kept hidden in secret places for fear of the pagans. Ilgar then found there, among the other relics in a marble capital which was hollowed out under the altar to serve as a tabernacle for the host, a little ball of the hair of Mary the holy mother of God. This he afterward took to France and shared out piously between the sanctuaries of the bishoprics and monasteries. . . . He gave two hairs to his kinsman the monk Arnold of Chartres and Arnold displayed them in the church of Maule where many sick persons have been cured through them.[31]

In his account to Anselm and Eadmer, Ilgra said that the hairs of the Virgin had been offered as a gift from a pious patriarch, but when Ordericus recorded the story as it had been told to him, they were part of a bribe for protection, taken by force from terrified local Christians. The two versions were meant for different audiences, and it is worth noticing the tone of piety in the version given to Anselm by a young soldier who knew him well. The procession with relics, and their deposition in various churches, showed widespread enthusiasm for them, but it was Eadmer not Anselm who kept and treasured the hairs as a permanent cause for wonder, though even Eamer was not entirely sure about them: 'what others feel about them I don't know.'

In his long meditation on the crucifixion, the *Prayer to Christ*, Anselm did not mention the legend behind the relics that Mary tore out her hair as she stood grieving by the cross. Anselm talked about her sufferings fervently but the image was not her hair but her tears, to which he joined his own. Weeping, sorrow of heart in which tears were seen as a renewal of the water of baptism, was a theological sorrow, and it was this that was of interest to him rather than external relics such as the hairs of the Virgin. The three long prayers to Mary with which Anselm took such pains contain his theology of Mary as the most powerful of intercessors – but no mention is made of her relics. However, the approach of the *Prayer to Christ*, which was among the most influential of Anselm's prayers and most clearly set the new emotional tone of meditation for the future, was very much a part of the sensual style of devotion to the hairs of the Virgin, as described by Eadmer in the words he ascribes to Ilgar:

'The Bishop of Antioch gave me twelve of them altogether, declaring that according to what, as he asserted, he found written in the records of ancient writings, which among them were held to be of great authority and were kept with the archives of the Church over which he presided, these hairs had been torn out by that Lady herself when, standing beside the cross of her Son, a sword pierced through her soul.'[32]

The new kind of personal emotion in the devotion of the eleventh century focused on the crucifixion, the details of the sufferings of Christ on the cross, rather than the theological significance of redemption. The humanity of the Virgin, her grief beside the cross, were therefore also explored, and depicted like the grief of a medieval woman, mourning, sobbing and tearing out her hair for sorrow. Legend further asserted that these hairs were collected by St John and preserved, as was the blood on the cross of Christ. The eagerness to have some tangible relic of Christ and of his mother, in spite of the fact that they were both believed to have been taken bodily into heaven at death, led to a zeal for any tangible fragments of parts of their bodies which had come off while they were alive. So there were relics of the blood Christ shed on the cross, the tears and hairs of the Virgin collected at the foot of the cross, as well as those that were linked to the other new focus of devotion, the Nativity, for example, the milk of the Virgin, shift and the slipper of the Virgin, milk teeth and umbilical cord of Christ. This approach appealed to Eadmer, and it was he who collected the hairs and kept them safely, not Anselm. It was Eadmer, not Anselm, who wrote passionately about the Virgin Mary in his defence of her immaculate conception. With all Anselm's profound devotion to Mary, it was not any relics of her that interested him, but her living heavenly friendship now.

The relics of another biblical saint were connected with Anselm, those of St Prisca. Eadmer described Anselm as confronted with the relics of a saint whose name is found six times in the New Testament (including as a variant, 'Priscilla').[33] Two sites in Rome claimed her interment. There can be queries about her and her links with the sites in Rome, but these were the questions of a later age. The transfer of the relics of the saints from Jerusalem, Constantinople and Rome to encourage the relic-less northern converts was a matter of fact; it had also aroused debate about the legitimacy of dividing the bones of saints in order to give them away. But the need to have relics of the apostles and martyrs and saints of the early Church predominated over the incongruity of having their bones scattered and therefore not together at the general resurrection. Eadmer was eager to have fragments of such bones and it was he who wrote about the offer of them made to Anselm:

During these proceedings, Walo bishop of Paris came to us. He was a man of sound religion and steeped in ecclesiastical customs and discipline from an early age. He was well-known at Rome where he had filled the office of papal legate and now enjoyed the friendship of father Anselm. He came to us then from Rome, and brought with him relics of certain saints, which – as we found out for certain – had been given to him at Rome. For when he was talking to Anselm in my presence, he told him what relics he had brought with him from Rome. At this Anselm gave thanks to God, and the bishop produced from a box a single bone which, he said, came from the head of the blessed martyr of God, Prisca. Explaining how he got it, he added: 'The church of this martyr, in which the altar was consecrated by Peter the most blessed Prince of the Apostles, was decayed and broken down with age. When I was in Rome, the body of the martyr was taken up so that a new church could be built. I was present at this, and since the cardinal of that church, who had charge of the saint's relics, was a friend of mine, he took this bone, which you see, from the holy body, and gave it to me as a token of our mutual affection.' The bishop stopped speaking; then drawn on by a love of having some of these relics I began to entreat the bishop to give me a piece of this body. 'Take it,' he said, 'and as much as you can break off at your first attempt shall be yours.' I took it and, behold, it turned out otherwise than I hoped: just as I began to pull, a piece came away in my right hand. When I was unable to hide my chagrin at its smallness and earnestly pressed him to allow me to break off another piece, Anselm broke off my petition. 'No, no', he said, 'Let what you have be sufficient for you. Truly, I tell you that the lady whose it is will not fail to claim it for herself in the day of general Resurrection, not for all the gold which is in Constantinople, or on this side of it, or beyond. Wherefore if you have treated it with proper reverence that will be as acceptable to her as if you had done so to her whole body.' When I heard this I was satisfied and to this day I have preserved the bone as decently as I could.[34]

Eadmer told the same story in his *History of Recent Events*.[35] He added the bone to his collection, but he was not quite satisfied about its provenance, or rather he wanted additional information to add to its glory; it may be that he was aware of a certain reservation about it in Anselm. For Anselm, one small fragment was the whole saint. For Eadmer, quantity was more than quality. For Anselm, the link with a saint in heaven was vital; for Eadmer, the need for reassurance about provenance on earth was what mattered. He did not leave the matter alone:

A long time afterwards Peter, a monk of Cluny and a man of great authority in his day being chamberlain of Popes Urban and Pascal, came to us and I asked him what he thought about this bone. When he heard my account of how I obtained it, he testified that everything the bishop had said about it was true, and he declared that he himself had been present when the bishop received the bone taken from the martyr's body by the cardinal.[36]

Anselm was connected with another saint of the early Church, St Nicholas, and for him he was ready to compose a long and complex prayer, but seems to have been totally uninterested in his relics in themselves, about whose historicity there were and are many queries. Nicholas ('great victor') was supposed in the eleventh century to have been the Bishop of Myra in the fourth century. The cult of Nicholas flourished as a patron of sailors long before Washington Irving turned him into the most popular of all saints as the New York 'Santa Claus' in the nineteenth century.[37] By Anselm's time, Nicholas had become immensely popular especially along the sea-boards of France and England. In 1087 the Norman 'translation' (seen by some as a simple theft) took place, with the removal of the relics of Nicholas from Myra to Bari and this may well have been the occasion that had caused Anselm to write his first draft of his long meditation addressed to St Nicholas. In 1093, he wrote to the monks at Bec and asked them to send this to him, perhaps in order to complete it or to send on with other prayers of his collection to those asking for such material. In the prayer, Anselm did not refer to the relics of Nicholas but to his miracles for the protection of the needy during his lifetime, and after his death he was called upon as a guide through purgatory and hell.[38] In his account of Anselm's presence at the Council of Bari, Eadmer twice mentioned pilgrims to the new and glorious shrine to St Nicholas which was a focus of interest, but Anselm seems not to have gone with them; it was Eadmer, not Anselm, who described it.

Nicholas was no new or local saint; he had been given a place in Latin calendars since the ninth century. Nor was the cult of St Nicholas a Norman importation into England; a thriving cult was there already among the Anglo-Saxons. Wulfstan of Worcester had been devoted to St Nicholas, even rivalling him in his care for sailors: 'In the seas between Bristol and Ireland, Wulfstan rivalled even St Nicholas as a protector of sailors during his life time.'[39] This was written by a disciple of Wulfstan who later wrote Wulfstan's life and changed his own name from Aethelstan to Nicholas. When the Normans invaded, a group of English nobles led by Siward had fled to Constantinople and established there a basilica dedicated jointly to St Nicholas and to St Augustine of Canterbury. There was some reason for Anselm to have shown interest in the tomb of Nicholas, as a saint of the early Church, as a figure in the universal calendar, as a saint specially respected at both Bec and Canterbury, but his only concern was with Nicholas as an intercessor in heaven for himself as a 'sinful little man, in such great need'.

These instances of the contact of Anselm with relics are meagre enough; and in each case what is revealed is Anselm's detachment from actual relics. The avid collection of relics was the fashion of the times, but whereas Eadmer, his close companion, was deeply involved in it, Anselm stood outside it. This was not a modern humanistic or automatic disbelief in their authenticity or their efficacy but an overwhelming primary interest in heavenly realities and values. He saw both the relic and the saint not as something valued for itself but as a part of the way to heaven for himself and all humankind. It is perhaps appropriate to note that the relics of Anselm himself received little recorded veneration and by the eighteenth century were subject to some contempt (see Chapter 6 below). His tomb did not become, like that of Becket, one of the major miracle-working places of the times, but his prayers continue to influence devotion throughout the world.

5

Canonization: Doctor Magnificus

———◆•◆•◆———

By 1200, the right to declare anyone a saint officially, and to recommend their name to be venerated by the whole Church, was being secured into the hands of the papacy.[1] The use of the term *canonizare* in the sense of official public recognition of a saint began in the eleventh century, meaning that the person concerned was placed in the canon of the Church's year and an annual liturgical commemoration on the anniversary of their death was sanctioned. This acknowledgement was sometimes accompanied by the removal of the bones to a more central position in the church (*translatio*). Before the eleventh century, this process was mainly in the hands of diocesan bishops, but it then gradually became the custom to ask for papal recognition of a new saint. The first official instance of papal canonization was that of Ulrich of Augsburg in 993; in 1170, a letter from Alexander III to Canute of Sweden asserted that no one should be publicly venerated as a saint without the authority of the Roman see; this became part of canon law.[2] This system increased the dignity of the proceeding and ensured a wider and more secure recognition beyond local and national borders. By 1200 this papal process had become a requirement and rules were formulated for the recognition of a saint. Finally, a long legal process was set out in the *Codex Juris Canonici* (canons 1999–2141). In order to deal with the vastly increasing business this meant outside the boundaries of a church council, a permanent committee (the Congregation of Rites) was established by Sixtus V in 1588, which in 1969 was divided into two, one of which was the Congregation for the Causes of the Saints.[3]

Anselm died at the moment when papal canonization was becoming the norm, but, almost by accident, what in effect he received was the older form of canonization, that by which someone would be acknowledged as a saint locally, by popular veneration for his holiness in life and death. Such a saint, whether locally or papally canonized, would normally have been venerated at his tomb, with miracles and visions occurring and offerings being made. While there are traces of such popular devotion to Anselm after his death, for instance in the 'guild of St Anselm',[4] his tomb did not become a major shrine with posthumous miracles and offerings and in this he remained outside the custom of his times. Moreover, his body became, in the eighteenth century, a focus for controversy of a kind quite unrelated to his life and thought. After Anselm's death in the archbishop's palace in Canterbury, his body was buried in the cathedral. His biographer Eadmer described the ceremony:

> And so he passed away as dawn was breaking on the Wednesday before the institution of the Lord's Supper, on 21 April in the year of our Lord's Incarnation 1109, which was the sixteenth year of his pontificate, and the seventy-sixth year of his life. . . . His body was washed according to custom and laid in a stone coffin. We anointed not only the hands and the head but also the arms and the breast and even his feet and the whole body in every part not just once but several times over. He was then clothed in his sacred vestments in the habit of an archbishop and carried into a chapel with the veneration due to him.[5]

A marginal note in a manuscript states that 'The venerable body of Father Anselm, Archbishop of Canterbury and primate of all Britain was shut in its (stone sarcophagus) sepulchre in the middle of the nave of the church near to Lanfranc'. This contemporary note indicates the first place of his burial, but it may in fact derive from Eadmer's account.

His burial near to Lanfranc was confirmed by William of Malmesbury, another Latin historian, and one who knew the works of Anselm and had once met him personally; he wrote, 'He was first buried at the head of his predecessor Lanfranc but was later given a worthier tomb in the east porch.'[6]

Ordericus Vitalis, writing at approximately that time, gave a different location: 'Finally, the good archbishop, dying on 21st. April went to receive the reward of his labours from the Lord, and was buried before the Rood in the church of the holy and undivided Trinity.'

Almost sixty years later, the body seems to have been moved, on 7 April 1168, to what is now called the Anselm Chapel. A twelfth-century MS of the Christ Church Calendar before 1171 contains the note: '7th April: Translatio Sancti Anselmi archiepiscopi et confessoris'.[7]

The translation of a saint's body to a new tomb was often an accompaniment to formal canonization, as well as a moment for offerings and miracles, but none of this seems to have been the case here; there is no other mention of this 'translation', until it was referred to six years later later in accounts of the fire in the cathedral in 1174 when it appears to have been a practical necessity: Gervase of Canterbury wrote in some detail in his *Tractatus de Combustione* and specifically mentioned Anselm:

> In the year of grace one thousand one hundred and seventy four, by the just but occult judgement of God, the church of Christ at Canterbury was consumed by fire . . . now the manner of the burning and repair was as follows: '. . . the altar of St Peter and St Paul. But St Anselm having been translated there and placed behind the altar gave his name to the altar and to the tower.'[8]

The next existing evidence came forty years later *c*.1315, in a 'List of Relics' compiled by Prior Henry Eastry (1315–16). Anselm's body is described in the list as 'in the shrine of S Peter'.[9] Since the altar in the Anselm Chapel was dedicated to Sts Peter and Paul, this seems to confirm the place of re-burial. The archbishop's coffin was probably at this time in a raised tomb beside or in front of the altar. His bones seem therefore to have rested in the Anselm Chapel throughout the Middle Ages.

When was Anselm himself counted officially as a saint? Eadmer suggests that he was regarded as a saint by many of those he encountered during his life. In 1098 during Anselm's exile and travels he encountered overwhelming honour. Before the Council of Bari, when he was in Italy, Eadmer says that he was so respected for holiness (*sanctitatis*) that 'even the pagans', Saracen soldiers who met and talked with him, thought him a saint. In Rome Anselm was honoured by the pope as 'apostolic patriarch of the other world' (*alterius orbis*, i.e. Britain). Eadmer says that later while at the Council of Rome, everyone in the city wanted his blessing and called him 'saint': 'hence scarcely anyone in Rome referred to him as "that man" or "that archbishop" but as if it were his own name, as "the saint" (*sanctus*)'.

This European respect for Anselm was not only for his pre-eminent learning but also for his behaviour: his *bonitas*, his wonderful kindness and his unassuming humility which made him approachable by all, a sure sign of sanctity. It is of course Eadmer who gives these details and part of his aim was to provide a 'hagio-graphy' (that is, a piece of writing about holiness) to show the likeness of Anselm to Christ, which is the basis of Christian sanctity. But Eadmer was also an historian and his two accounts of Anselm can also be seen as records of earthly events more in the line of the 'bio-graphy' (a piece of writing about earthly life) which has become the style of modern accounts of people. While there were certainly those who opposed Anselm and his opinions on many matters, his personal conduct does not seem to have been seriously questioned. This common assumption that Anselm was a saint may be held to be sufficiently attested and seems to have continued tranquilly after his death so that his reputation as a saint was permanent but low-key. The only English church outside Canterbury where there is unambiguous evidence for the liturgical observance of the day of his death is St Werburgh's, Chester, which was a daughter house of Bec. At Canterbury itself his reputation grew slowly and was soon eclipsed by the fame of St Thomas Becket.

Another contemporary writer besides Eadmer who considered Anselm a saint was John of Salisbury, who wrote another account of his life, briefer than that of Eadmer and more streamlined towards the new requirements about canonization. Another Archbishop of Canterbury, Theobald, made a distinction in his letters between Lanfranc and Anselm; Lanfranc was '*bonae memoriae*' or '*piae recordationis*', while Anselm was '*sanctus*' or '*sanctissimae memoriae*'.[10] But there is no reason to think that there was any liturgical commemoration of Anselm even at Canterbury until the time of Archbishop Thomas Becket. In the calendar of *Eadwine's Psalter*, Anselm's day was marked with the simple notice, '*ob. piae memoriae Anselmus archiepiscopus*'.[11]

With the coming of Thomas Becket as archbishop a great change took place, since Becket was known for his admiration of Anselm. It seems that the formal canonization of Anselm was proposed by Becket at the Council of Tours in 1163 but when this request with its summary of evidence reached Alexander III he was harassed by a large number of similar demands. He therefore placed them all on hold until there was more leisure to consider them. A letter he wrote after the council to Archbishop Thomas Becket throws light upon the special status of Anselm as well as the situation as regards papal control of canonization:

Bishop Alexander, servant of the servants of God, to his venerable brother Thomas, archbishop of Canterbury, greetings and apostolic blessings. When you were in our presence, you humbly and devotedly petitioned us to canonize Anselm of holy memory, former archbishop of Canterbury, whose life and miracles you presented to us at the council of Tours. Since there were many others there who were urgently seeking the same thing on behalf of other holy men, we thought fit to defer your request in order to avoid the scandal of envy. Now however with complete confidence in your integrity and prudence in all things, we entrust the matter to your care and discretion, and command you by apostolic letter to summon into your presence our brothers, your suffragan bishops, together with the abbots and other religious persons of your province, and after solemnly reading the life of that holy man and publically proclaiming hid miracles in their presence, you may proceed with the support of our authority to carry out the findings of the council in respect of his canonization with the advice and consent of the brethren there present, in the knowledge that we shall, by the Lord's will, ratify and confirm whatever you and the aforesaid brothers decide in this matter. Given at Tours 9th June 1163.[12]

Thomas Becket had been present at the Council of Tours along with Roger the Archbishop of York, and in fact had disputed with him there about a matter of Canterbury and York precedence that arose between them. From the tone of this letter it seems that Alexander had confidence in Becket. In a time when canonization was increasingly falling into the hands of the papacy, he gave Becket a mandate to canonize Anselm. Sufficient material in *The Life of St Anselm* (either that by Eadmer or possibly that of John of Salisbury) with his miracles (*vita et miracula*) had been presented at Tours with the request for a canonization, but so many other applicants had appeared, including an application from the Cistercian order for consideration of a massive amount of material relating to Bernard of Clairvaux, that the Pope had postponed them all; there was too much work involved, and canonization now needed discussion apart from the business of a general council. The Pope was ready to recognize Anselm as a saint but he did not want to make an exception at the Council by canonizing Anselm only, as he says, in case promoting only one might make the others cross. The implication is that he himself was confident about Anselm, and indeed the close alliance of Anselm and the papacy and the affection and respect felt for him in Rome were potent factors. In this letter to Becket, the earlier pattern of local canonization by acclamation and approval by the local bishops is implied, and indeed this seems to have been the case since this was the only official papal document for the canonization of Anselm.

Becket was involved in more pressing matters within a few months of his return to England and, as far as records go, the matter was taken no further. His own death and swift canonization may well have taken interest at all levels away from his less colourful predecessor. However, Anselm's name appeared in a calendar of Christ Church, Canterbury, which can be dated before 1171, with his feast day on the anniversary of his death, 21 April, and 7 April as the day of his translation:

7 april translatio sancti anselmi archiepiscopi et confessoris
21 april festivitas gloriosissimi patris nostri Anselmi archiepiscopi et confessoris.[13]

The title of 'saint' suggests that Anselm was by then accepted into the calendar of the saints with or without a local English council. There also must have been a translation, though this need not imply official recognition.

There are remarkably few references to a cult of St Anselm thereafter. King Stephen made a grant of land in Kent to support a light burning before the 'capsa of S Anselm' which can be tentatively dated 1153–54, 'capsa' maybe indicating a shrine rather than the original sarcophagus.[14] Dr Urry had listed several charters and also identified the members of a local Canterbury

'Guild of St Anselm'; it had at one point 135 members which dwindled and died out.[15]

The matter lapsed in official circles and indeed was overtaken by the martyrdom of Becket in 1170, his speedy canonization in 1173 and the outburst of devotion to his tomb and his relics, making Canterbury one of the chief shrines of Christendom.

> It may still have been hoped to bring the process of canonization to a successful conclusion. But . . . after this date, there seems never again to have been any question of formal canonization, or any new examination of the record of Anselm's life for this purpose. His name did not appear in the *Martyrologium secundum more in Romanae curiae 100* of 1498, nor in the revised editions of this work before 1568. But in the new edition of the Roman Martyrology made by John Molanus of Louvain in this year, there appeared among the additions in italics under 21 April, this entry:
>
> *Sancti Anselmi episcopi Cantuariensis et confessoris*
>
> A note to the entry gave a reference to Eadmer's *Life.* . . . The sources of Molanus's additions were largely the calendars of Belgian churches, and Gravius's edition of the *Life.* . . . It would appear, therefore, that Anselm owed his inclusion in the Roman Martyrology to the diffusion of his fame in Flanders, where Eadmer's biography had gained an early popularity. Anselm retained his place in the Roman Martyrology when it was officially revised under Gregory XIII, and from this time it was never assailed.[16]

Anselm was proclaimed a Doctor of the Church ('*Doctor Magnificus*', a phrase coined originally by Peter Abelard) in 1720 by Pope Clement XI.[17] The monastic office for the feast of St Anselm had already been approved by the Congregation of Rites in 1703, and Pope Clement XI, at the request of 'James III, King of Great Britain, etc.', raised the status of his feast. Eight hundred years after his death, on 21 April 1909,

Pope Pius X issued an encyclical *Communium Rerum* praising Anselm, his ecclesiastical career, and his writings. The anniversary of Anselm's death on 21 April is now celebrated in the Roman Catholic Church, the Anglican Communion, and the Lutheran Church as Anselm's memorial day. It seems that Anselm has been recognized as among the saints in an unemotional and unobtrusive fashion which fits well with his character and career.

6

Anselm's relics

————◆◆◆————

Part of the centralization of the process of canonization had to do with regulating the increasing trade in false relics. As well as an overwhelming care for the bones of the saints, there had always been some criticism of mercenary tricks connected with relics. Augustine of Hippo, while advocating the veneration of the relics of St Stephen, had also complained of the sale of fraudulent relics in the fourth century: '[The devil] has dispensed on every side so many hypocrites, under the garb of monks strolling about the provinces, nowhere sent, nowhere settled, nowhere standing, nowhere sitting. Some hawk about the limbs of martyrs, if indeed they be martyrs.'[1]

Guibert of Nogent in the first half of the twelfth century maintained the value of relics for popular devotion while strictly condemning fraud and superstition; especially he was offended by the breaking up of the bodies of the dead, and their use for gain, without investigation of their provenance: 'What is a wise and modest man who professes a resolution of sanctity doing to encourage such things?'[2]

Bernard of Clairvaux adopted a similar stance, turning from external exposition of relics towards an interiorization of devotion through them. This concern for inner faith went so far that it could be preferred to reality: in the cult of St Thomas at Canterbury, Benedict of Peterborough, in his account of Becker's miracles, says that when a sick man was urgently in need of the mixture of water and the blood of Thomas which was offered as a prophylactic and none could be obtained quickly, ordinary water was given him, with the comment that it would work just as well where there was faith.[3]

In all this there was no doubt about the power of the saints through their bones. But in the sixteenth century there was a change in the kind of criticism made of relics. It was no longer that they might in some instances be fraudulent or used for gain: the nature of a relic was under attack as well. It seems that the action of the government and their ecclesiastical advisors in England in the sixteenth century in taking relics out of their shrines, re-burying them, and forbidding veneration of them, was influenced partly by cupidity, but largely by the new thinking of the Protestant world which was making its mark. The priority of the Scriptures, and the stress on direct access to God, made the cult of saints and especially of their relics seem indeed a 'fond thing vainly invented', and the jeers of those who suggested that the 'bones' were often not even human remains but those of animals added further doubts. Luther (1483–1546) criticized the cult of relics as being unnecessary and without warrant of Scripture[4] but the two sixteenth-century writers who attacked relics in the most sustained and the most influential way were the Catholic Erasmus (1469–1536) and the Protestant Calvin (1509–64). By examining their writings on the subject in the *Pilgrimage for Religion's Sake* of Erasmus,[5] and the *Traite des Reliques* of John Calvin,[6] it is possible to see the kind of opposition to relics there was from two different views of Christian life, and so to understand the mental climate in which this devotion could fall away with so little protest, setting the stage for the eighteenth-century's violent opposition to the relics of Anselm.

Erasmus (1469–1536), a humanist and a Catholic, aimed the barb of mockery at the cult of relics in his colloquy, *A Pilgrimage for Religion's Sake*. It circulated in 1518, apparently on the initiative of others. Erasmus certainly knew Luther's opinions, as well as those of the Swiss Protestant Zwingli (1484–1531); indeed in his tract the name 'Glaucoplutus' (Owl-rich) may have been a play on the first name of Ulrich Zwingli; and when Erasmus was censured for this work by the Sorbonne he declared that it was directed against the Zwinglians. 'Glaucoplutus' was presented as the recipient of a letter, replete with irony, written as from the Virgin Mary, thanking him for saving her work and worry by 'busily persuading people that the invocation of saints is useless'. Erasmus' weapon was a fine satirical approach throughout but it is useful to see what he was in fact attacking. The colloquy is set in the form of a dialogue between Menedemus and Ogygius (Erasmus), in which the former interrogates the latter about supposed pilgrimages to St James at Compostela and Our Lady of Walsingham, the great Marian shrine in Norfolk. Written in elegant Latin, it was first printed in 1526 and translated into English by an anonymous writer in 1536, the year of the dissolution of the monasteries in England, and circulated under the title *The Pilgrimage of Pure Devotion*. It became a valuable piece of propaganda which Thomas Cromwell was ready to see published and circulated. Many of the ideas of the Protestant theologians here found elegant and readable form, from a person acceptable with both Catholics and the English Reformers and *literati*; the elegant scorn of Erasmus combined with the new theology entered the mental atmosphere of the times and expressed a new way of thinking which proved destructive of the cult of relics, beyond the expectations and wishes of Erasmus himself.

Erasmus poked fun at those who behaved foolishly either in presenting false relics for veneration or in misusing them in a stupid and self-seeking way. It is ridicule directed against relics, but within it Erasmus presented the possibility of a sober and devout reverence for the saints which strikes a less radical note than the Reformers while appealing to the same desire for an end to fraud and frivolity. He had himself visited the shrine of Our Lady of Walsingham in 1512 and 1514 and the shrine of St Thomas at Canterbury with John Colet in the same years. The mercenary motives of some of those who visited shrines and petitioned saints were exposed with elegant wit: he wrote in the same satirical letter from Mary:

> Sometimes a merchant off to Spain to make a fortune, commits to me the chastity of his mistress. A nun who has thrown off her veil and is preparing to run away entrusts me with her reputation for virtue – which she herself meant to sell . . . an unmarried girl cries, 'Mary, give me a rich and handsome husband'; a married woman, 'Give me fine children' . . . a doddering old man, 'Let me grow young again'.

Ridicule was also thrown upon unlikely relics such as a beam on which the Virgin once stood, or her milk, but genuine contempt was heaped upon avaricious and slovenly guardians of shrines; with the arrogance of the first scholar of Europe, Erasmus had particular scorn for canons at shrines who did not recognize Greek letters when they saw them. But this was not to deny that right reverence might and indeed should be paid to the saints. Erasmus wrote a poem in Greek for Our Lady of Walsingham and had it placed in the shrine. His colloquy contained prayers which were a model of devotion to a saint, purged but nonetheless ardent. He wrote:

> When I entered the chapel [at Walsingham] I greeted the Virgin Mother with a short payer like this: 'O thou alone of all womankind mother and virgin, Mother most blessed, purest of maidens, we who are unclean come to thee who art pure. We bless thee, we worship thee as best we can with our poor gifts. May thy Son grant us that, by emulating thy most blessed life, we too, through the grace of the Holy Spirit, may be made worthy to conceive the Lord Jesus Christ spiritually in our hearts and never lose him once conceived.' Kissing altar at the same time, I laid some coins upon it and went away.

With John Calvin, the criticism of the cult of relics left the realm of mockery from within belief for the arena of outright condemnation in principle. Calvin crystallized his criticism of relics in 1543 at a time when he was reaffirming his authority in Geneva. Reissued the following year, in 1548 the *Traite des Reliques* was translated into the international language of Latin for wider circulation. Between 1552 and 1667 it was translated five times into Latin, into German, into Dutch and, in 1561, into English, where it bore the title:

> A very profitable Treatise, declarying what great profit might come to all Christendom yf there were a register made of all the saints' bodies and other reliques which are as well in Italy as in France, Dutchland, Spain and all kingdoms and countreys. Translated out of the French into English by J. Wythers, London, 1561.

Like all Calvin's works, it reached an eager, newly literate, audience. It is written with a certain savage humour which perhaps made it more popular than more strictly theological works. It took up many of the abuses which Erasmus had satirized gently in order to induce a sensible reform, and denounced them with a merciless hand. Many of the vivid images and satirical comments and observations of the *Traite* entered into the consciousness of educated people and have remained there ever since.

What was Calvin criticizing in the *Traite*? He began with a reference to Augustine of Hippo, in order to give his arguments the appearance of the authority of the early Church, and referred to Augustine's protests against the fraudulent relics offered by the unscrupulous for veneration of the simple (see p. 81). He then expressed the view that Christianity has declined vastly since then, and had now reached a point where people were more interested in relics, false or otherwise, than in the plain teaching of Christ. Thus, his first objection was against deception and fraud; his second protest was against idolatry; and his third argument was to suggest that the possession of relics of the saints in itself was bound to produce idolatry. He combined this with the first point, by suggesting that such idolatry is not only shameful but foolish, since the relics were probably not what they were asserted to be. Calvin admitted that venerable Christians of the past, such as St Helena the mother of Constantine, had both possessed relics that were true relics and had venerated Christ all the more by their means. But this, he said, was rare to the point of being unique. He was not, therefore, he continued, saying that relics, true relics, were not in themselves venerable objects, but that men were too corrupt, too full of avarice, to use them for their salvation. Such caution was surely a literary device to disarm opponents who continued to support veneration for the saints, by seeming not to reject the veneration in itself, but only the two forms of abuse to which it was open: fraud and idolatry. The rest of the book was presented as a factual account of the relics Calvin had seen during his visits to France, Germany, Spain and Italy, and in particular those near Geneva. To these relics he proposed the questions: were they what they are claimed to be? Were they historically and sometimes were they practically what they seemed? His answer in each case was 'no'. The effect was to make the reader feel that belief was not so much sinful as foolish, the most telling of all forms of criticism.

Calvin attacked supposed relics of Christ, of the Virgin Mary, of the apostles and of later saints. They were not, could not be, what they claimed to be; and what was more, even if they were authentic, 'the desire for relics is never without superstition . . . usually it is the parent of idolatry.' His criticism was the same as that of Luther, who wrote, 'What lies there are about relics! One man claims to possess a feather from the wing of the angel Gabriel and the bishop of Mainz has a flame from Moses's burning bush.'[7] Such questions came from a change in perception of reality: the validity of something now depended on its provenance, not its usefulness; the question, 'what is this for?' was replaced by the question 'how does this work?' The new ideas were therefore welcomed as being undoubtedly true in the sense of being 'scientific'.

A humble, loving devotion to the saints had, it seems, been right in the eyes of a Catholic sixteenth-century humanist, a writer with as much scholarly skill as Calvin. The ridicule and scorn of the Reformers for falsehood is there in Erasmus, but in this, as in other matters, he discerned a middle way between the outright rejection of saints and their relics in principle, and the continuance of old ways, purified and rationalized. This could have prevented what in fact happened, the cult of the saints becoming a part of the militant reaction of Catholics against Protestants. Erasmus was for a purified cult, with fraud and selfishness purged from it, leading to the ends of the Reformers, 'discerning Jesus in his word, sacraments and spiritual graces', but without rejecting the ways of the past. But it was the destructive approach of Calvin which triumphed.

The ground for change was prepared in the intellectual world of Erasmus, Luther and Calvin. Politics then made use of the theories. In the sixteenth century, the criticism of saints' cults caused a major change to the English religious world by the abolition of all shrines in England; its terms can be most clearly seen in the decree of Henry VIII issued in 1541:

> We did not only cause [i.e., in 1538] the images and bones of such as they restored and offered unto, with the ornaments of the same, and all such writings and monuments of fained miracles, wherewith they were deluded, to be taken away in all places of our realm but also by our injunctions commanded that no offering or setting of lights or candles should be suffered in any church but only to the blessed sacrament of the altar.[8]

It was veneration of shrines that was forbidden: Protestants were as keen as Catholics to respect the bodies of the dead, and would naturally have reburied those extracted from shrines. Letters indicate that while treasures from the shrines were conveyed to the Tower of London, in many cases, notably those of

Hugh of Lincoln, Cuthbert of Durham, Richard of Chichester
and William of York, the bones were reburied on or near the
site of the shrine. The case of Thomas Becket was not typical,
since he was especially the subject of the King's personal ani-
mosity. In Oxford, the bones of St Frideswide were removed
from the shrine in the late 1530s and reburied on the site.
Catherine Dammorin, the wife of the Protestant Reformer,
Peter Martyr Vermigli, canon of Christ Church and the first
Regius Professor of Divinity, was buried 'near the tomb of St
Frideswide' in 1552; exhumed in 1556 by Queen Mary's com-
missioners, she was buried again in 1561, together with two silk
bags containing the supposed relics of St Frideswide, acciden-
tally also unearthed. An observer wrote:

> I hit upon a scheme by which the bones could be dealt with
> decently while at the same time all foolish superstition could
> be suppressed . . . they were mingled with the bones of Peter
> Martyr's wife in the upper part of the church towards the east,
> in the same monument, much honoured and frequented by
> men, on Jan. 11th 1561.[9]

It seems highly likely therefore that the bones of St Anselm
were removed from their container and reburied in the same
way in the Anselm Chapel.

The influence of the Reformation's criticism of relics is
apparent in the next mention of Anselm's bones. The ambi-
guity in Anselm's life continued after his death. In spite of the
lack of official recognition as a saint, Anselm had clearly been
regarded as a holy person in his life as well as at his death, and
respect for his writings grew constantly, but veneration of his
bones always seems to have been at a minimum. They were not
so much criticized as ignored until the eighteenth century.
Then an unexpected request to the Archbishop of Canterbury
gave rise to some extremely adverse remarks about Anselm's
relics; they are perhaps the most extreme comments in scorn
of relics anywhere or at any time.

Thomas Herring (1693–1757) was Archbishop of Canterbury from 1747 to 1757. At Jesus College, Cambridge, he was a contemporary of Matthew Hutton, who succeeded him in turn in each of his dioceses. He received his MA in 1717 and was a fellow at Corpus Christi College Cambridge from 1716 to 1723. Herring became a close friend of Philip Yorke, the Solicitor General, who would later, as Lord Hardwicke, serve for many years as Lord Chancellor; as his protégé, Herring was able to advance quickly. In 1728 he became Doctor of Divinity and was appointed as a chaplain to George II. In 1737 he was made Bishop of Bangor. Six years later he became Archbishop of York, where he organized opposition to the Jacobite rising of 1745 and in 1747 he became, although reluctantly, Archbishop of Canterbury. There he generally followed the lead of his friend the Lord Chancellor, and frequently came into disputes with the Duke of Newcastle, the Secretary of State. Herring's inclination was to support the Hanoverian side in disputes but as archbishop he saw himself as a conciliator and claimed that he eschewed controversy and felt that he was 'called up to this high station, at a time when spite and rancour and bitterness of spirit are out of countenance; when we breathe the benign and comfortable air of liberty and toleration'.[10] He was a rationalist, and therefore totally scornful of superstition of all kinds, but in his way he was a devout man, and was the author of *A New Form of Common Prayer*, published anonymously in 1753. 'The benign and comfortable air of liberty and toleration' was not, however, apparent in the tone he adopted in his letter to the Dean of Canterbury about Anselm's relics:

Dear Mr Dean

I had a request communicated to me today of a very singular nature; it comes from the ambassador of a great Catholic prince. Archbishop Anselm it seems lies buried in our cathedral, and the King of Sardinia (Victor Emmanuel) has a great desire to be possessed of his bones, or dust and coffin. It seems he was of the county of Aosta, the bishop of which has put this desire into the king's head, who by the by, is a most prodigious bigot, and in a late dispute with Geneva gave up territory to redeem an old church. You will please to consider this request with your friends but not yet in chapter. You will believe I have no great scruples upon this head, but if I had I would get rid of them all, if the parting with the rotten remains of a rebel to his king, a slave to the popedom and an enemy to the married clergy (all this Anselm was) would purchase ease and indulgence to one living Protestant. It is believed that a condescension in this business may facilitate the way of doing it to thousands. I think it is worth the experiment and really for this end I make no conscience of palming on the simpletons any other old bishop with the name of Anselm. (Dec. 23rd 1752)[11]

Herring's response was not only caused by his theological opinions. He was not only a convinced and rational Protestant, he was also a firm supporter of the house of Hanover and there were Jacobite strands within the source of the request. Charles Emmanuel III, 1730–73, was a grandson of Henrietta Anne Stuart, youngest sister of Charles I. Herring's view of Anselm as 'a rebel to his king, a slave to the popedom and an enemy to the married clergy' was in line with other descriptions, notably the comments of John Foxe.

The matter was not allowed to drop as Herring obviously hoped it would have done; he wrote a further letter to Dean Lynch two weeks later:

Dear Mr Dean

Count Perron has been with me just now, and signified his master, the K. of Sardinia's request as to the coffin and bones of archb. Anselm. The count is desirous to apply to the Dean and Chapter of Canterbury in the most respectful manner, and most agreeable to them. Upon which subject I told him I would consult you. The count intimated, that if anything is found and a removal made, it will be necessary for him to be upon the spot, an ocular witness in order to testify in the most authentical manner the reality of this precious deposit. I suppose the old tomb has ponderous and marble jaws so that it will make some noise to effect this important work; be sure you have no Protestant vergers that can look upon this as Diana of the Ephesians. This you will consider. I have said nothing to the Count, but declared your and my readiness . . . (Jan. 6th 1753)

Count Perron was envoy extraordinary and minister plenipotentiary of the King of Sardinia, and was suspicious of the attitude of the English he had to deal with; he was ready to take great care by his presence not to be duped by the actions of Canterbury in this matter.

This was followed by a letter from 'S.S.', probably Samuel Shuckford, writer and author of *The Sacred and Profane History of the World*. He became a prebendary of Canterbury at this time, and as an historian close at hand he had been consulted by the dean. He wrote thereafter to Archbishop Herring:

May it please your Grace, I should have sooner acknowledged the receipt of your Grace's appointment for me to preach at Whitehall Mar. 30th which duty I shall be careful to attend, but that the Dean has this day or two taken up my thought with two letters of your Grace concerning Abp. Anselm. I went yesterday morning by his order with your letters to the prebendaries, to ask them to meet the Dean capitularly to agree a search. But Dr Holcolme, Dr Ayerd, and Dr Walwyn are confined at home by indispositions, that we cannot at present meet in any one place. The Dean told me just now, that he intended to write to your Grace to have the affair a little deferred. As this will occasion some stop in the proceedings, I beg your Grace will give me leave to submit to your Grace what I think I find concerning Anselm.

He was first buried about a.d. 1109 at the head of his predecessor Abp Lanfranc, who though afterwards removed, was at first laid on the south side of the altar of the Holy Trinity, in what was then called Trinity Chapel, afterwards called St Thomas (à Becket's) chapel. Upon the new building of this part of the church both Lanfranc and Anselm were taken up: Lanfranc was I think deposited at St Martin's altar, which seems to have been in a rotund niche in the north cross aisle in the upper part of the church. Anselm was buried in a chapel called by his own name, near the altar of St Peter and St Paul. Afterwards I think Hen 7. time: he was canonized, had a shrine and the name of St Peter and St Paul's Altar was changed to St Anselm's Altar. I suppose he was now taken up again and his relics put into the shrine. And surely this new shrine and its contents as Becket's shrine and all other shrines were disposed of at the Reformation. I should hence think it impracticable to find St Anselm's coffin, dust or bones.

All this I hinted to the Dean and took the liberty to say further that I feared our undercroft had since the Reformation been in so neglected a state that I could not say that it could be even desirable to have a foreign personage in high character take the offence at our manner of using it which his coming to have an ocular inspection and examination of it would surely give one of his Communion.

Thus far I have gone with the Dean: I say no more for he seemed not to be pleased with me, but I venture to offer to your Grace's inspection what was further in my mind. Whether, though I am sure it cannot be found: the searching for to authenticate in the manner designed one who was canonized, had his altar, and his day of service, I think it was the 23rd of May, may not be considered in a further view than that of looking for the remains of an old Abp only to be removed and be deposited in his native country. I hope I do not offend your Grace herein and may humbly beg my perhaps very injudicious sentiment may be confined only to your Grace's favourable thoughts of me, for I should not desire to venture it for the censure of anyone more severe than I am sure your Grace will be to me. I am may it please your Grace with the greatest sincerity of duty your Grace's most obedient and humble servant S.S. (Canterbury Jan 9th 1753)

Shuckford presented a hasty, vague and at times wrong version of the history of Anselm's remains, but at least he was aware that there was a case to be answered. The clerical dovecotes at the cathedral seem to have taken this request badly and the Archbishop was not overwhelming in his reception of the idea of a historical hunt for the relics either. It is interesting that the crypt was mentioned as the obvious place where one would expect to look for relics, and the state of the crypt at Canterbury can be deduced from Shuckford's hint.

Apparently Shuckford was not the only antiquarian to be stirred by the request. The next letter from Archbishop Herring to the Dean introduced another scholar into the fray, but this time the researches had been conducted more thoroughly and for the benefit of those asking for the relics.

Dear Mr Dean,
The inclosed was put into my hands which I transmit to your inspection. I know you will give it all due and reverend consideration. Who this antiquarian Bradley is, I know not. I am, dear sir, your most assured friend April 14th 1753

The enclosure was a long and detailed account of Anselm's relics:

London 31st March 1753 P. Bradley to Count Perron
To Count Perron. My Lord,
In compliance with your Lordship's orders, no pains have been spared by me in consulting and examining all such antiquarians and historians as might give me the least intimation where Anselm's reliques were deposited and might to this day be preserved; the result of which is a full persuasion that St Anselm's body lies in the tomb vulgarly called Theobald's posterior to Anselm about an hundred years only and whose body anno 1180 after the fire was translated into the nave of the church and deposited at the altar of the blessed Virgin, from whence by anything I can find it was never after removed . . . see Battely from Gervais' History of the Church cap. IV p. 5. About 400 years after Anselm's death, Archbishop Morton ad 1487 procured him to be canonized. Long before this Malmesbury (I cannot readily find in what age he lived) speaking of the

removal of St Anselm from the head of Lanfranc says 'dignius mausoleum accepit in orientali porticu' which answers to that of Theobald's erroneously so called. Battely speaks doubtingly 'and laid (viz. after his removal) I take it,' says he, 'in the chapel yet bearing his name' (p. 122) whereas Somner, much the abler historian, is positive that Theobald's mistaken tomb is really St Anselm's. Battely himself owns a mistake about Theobald's tomb caused by the authority of the Protestant archbishop Godwin, who buries him in the south part of St Thomas's chapel, in a marble joining to the wall; and accordingly, says Battely, there hangs a table lately made of him (Theobald) and his acts; but by what authority I can't guess; for I am sure that none that have wrote his life before abp Godwin have authorized this report. Besides another improbabiliy that it should be Theobald's is its having not inscription as Theobald's had, for which I refer to Weaver. Whose then could it be but Anselm's? Somner was a great Kentish antiquarian and is of the opinion that the tomb of bishop Theobald is falsely ascribed to him and is in reality that of St Anselm's. And upon the strictest inquiry I do not find him contradicted by any authority but that of archbishop Godwin. For Theobald's reputed tomb though at a little distance is really 'retro altare sancti Anselmi' where or near which resteth his body. The chapel is as contiguous to the said monument as, considering the fabric of the church, it could be placed; in the chapel the lamps before the altar were posterior to his canonization and had no connection with the removal of the body from the 'dignius mausoleum' mentioned by Malmesbury, and consequently much less with the demolition of it, in order to place the body only a few paces nearer to the altar and the lights before it. I have therefore a strong presumption on my side to believe St Anselm's remains are in Theobald's tomb. If your excellency will obtain his Grace the archbishop of Canterbury's leave to remove the side of the tomb and inspect it, I hope my opinion grounded on so good an authority, will turn out to your satisfaction. In the scrutinium as the acts call it or opening of St Dunstan's monument by archbshop Wareham (see Battely's appendix to his first part) a 'lamina plumbea' was found on the saint's body inclosed in two leaden and one wooden coffin hooped with iron, inscribed with his name in Roman letters. Matthew Paris says that this was the custom in those days, epitaphs being of a posterior date. If we should not meet with any such thing, denoting the body of Anselm to lie there, the whole affair would be over at a small expense and all other search unnecessary; till then I beg leave to be sanguine enough to believe him still there and really cannot conclude otherwise; it being impossible I think that the saint's remains and mausoleum should have been destroyed and no notice taken of it either by Catholic or Protestant writers. I should think myself extremely happy if the pains I have taken to contribute towards his Majesty's and your Excellency's pious zeal to promote the worship of saints should prove efficient on this occasion. All I can take upon me at present to hint to your excellency is that upon obtaining the grace of Canterbury's orders to open and visit Theobald's supposed tomb, it ought to be done with as much secrecy as possible and at a time when the church doors are shut; otherwise the country being alarmed the mob would rush in and there would be nothing but confusion. The opening of St Dunstan's tomb by Archbishop Wareham was performed in the night and required two whole nights before it was completed; then the proctors etc were sent for and affidavits made in due form. The same method might be pursued in the affair in question. I wish it were in my power to render further service to your Excellency none would be more willing or esteem himself more honoured by it than my Lord your excellency's most humble obedient servant P. Bradley. (London 31st March 1753)

It seems that Count Perron had employed a Catholic to explore the matter, the man called Bradley, about whom nothing more seems to be known, who dutifully read several printed books about the cathedral and Anselm, such as Somner's *Antiquities of Canterbury*, Battley's *Cantuaria Sacra* and Weaver's *Funeral Memorials*. He does not seem to have visited Canterbury and added nothing new to what was already known, but summarized it for his patron, coming to the conclusion that Anselm's bones were then to be found in the Anselm Chapel in the tomb there attributed to Theobald and later to Hubert Walter. The matter seems to have been abandoned there, possibly because the count was, with good reason, suspicious of the response of Canterbury and did not want to risk being given fakes.

The conclusions I draw from these letters is that there was a sincere and traditional desire for the relics of Anselm in at least two Catholic countries. They ventured cautiously to ask a Protestant nation for them. However, they were on the look out for trickery and insisted on seeing the recovery of the relics personally. There was a cynical and indeed mocking note in the reception of this by Archbishop Herring, who did not hold with relics at all, and when told a bit about Anselm was equally dismissive of him. The Protestant slant of Herring's politics made him especially unfavourable towards any Catholic predecessor and he held Anselm to have been politically wrong in opposing two kings. The links of the King of Sardinia with the house of Stuart and the fact that the canonization of Anselm was being proposed by 'James III' in Herring's mind connected him with the Jacobites whom he had been instrumental in defeating in 1745. Also, in line with Calvin, he was so scornful of the whole idea of relics that he was prepared for any kind of fake if it would secure privileges for Protestants abroad. The tone of his letter was uncouth and earned a low-key rebuke from even the sycophantic Shuckford:

> Whether though I am sure it cannot be found: the searching for to authenticate in the manner designed one who was canonized, had his altar, and his day of service, . . . may not be considered in a further view [i.e., with a more serious attitude] than that of looking for the remains of an old Abp only to be removed and be deposited in his native country.

In this moment when the relics of Anselm were in question, no progress was made. There was caution in the deanery at

Canterbury and scornful non-involvement from the Archbishop. The chance that the deplorable state of the crypt might be revealed to the eyes of foreigners made them all particularly thoughtful. Two antiquarians who were asked to explore the matter did so, one for Sardinia, one for Canterbury. But they tailored their findings in view of the politics of each side. In the English replies, there was no trace of devotion or a desire for any discovery or authentication of relics; they are as far from the past by their prejudices as we are by our own. No doubt there was a sense that the bodies of the dead should be treated with respect, but they held by the Prayer Book injunction that any 'lifting up or carrying around' of bones should be avoided and was indeed mocked as superstition for the ignorant. The serious wishes of the Catholic princes Victor Emmanuel and Victor Amadeus was to the clergy of Canterbury both incomprehensible and laughable. As in his lifetime, in the view of Anselm taken by later ages, politics certainly had its part to play in the kind of contempt heaped on his memory. Throughout his life, Anselm's strong alliance with the papacy and the tenets of the Gregorian Reform had brought him into disagreement with both kings and clerics over both the married status of the clergy and the desire of the state to limit the authority of Rome. These issues were also prominent again at the Reformation. Anselm's quarrels with two kings were seen by some of his contemporaries, but even more by English politicians of the eighteenth century, especially those loyal to the house of Hanover, as treasonous on a political level. In such ways the concerns of their times coloured their view of the past and limited their approach to facts, thereby producing a distorted idea of one of the most scholarly and devout of men.

Three-quarters of a century later, another letter raised the matter again of the relics of Anselm.

1814. 'Lord Bolton'[12] 'to a friend at Canterbury' [perhaps W. R. Lyall, canon and afterwards Dean of Canterbury]

My Dear Sir,

I have lately been applied to from Turin to procure some information respecting the remains of an archbishop of Canterbury named Anselm who lived under the reign of William Rufus and was a native of Piedmont. Having heard that you have become an inhabitant of the above named city and that you are connected with the chapter of its cathedral and having moreover often experienced your kind and obliging disposition, I venture to trouble you with the request that you will ascertain for me whether the archbishop Anselm was buried in Canterbury Cathedral or in any where in the city or whether the place containing his remains is separate and distinguishable in such a manner as to be pointed out or removed. You will feel much surprised at these odd and extraordinary questions, but I doubt whether your surprise will exceed mine on the subject. I have a great mind to have run down myself to Canterbury to make a verbal call on your good nature but the weather has prevented me, and I am now obliged much to my regret to entrust this letter with my communication. With best wishes and regards I remain, my dear sir, yours sincerely, Bolton, 11, Grosvenor Street, August 16th 1814.

Presumably this enquiry came from Victor Emmanuel. No reply survives to suggest that any further action was undertaken.[13]

7

Anselm today

It remains to ask what value a discussion of Anselm in relation to his prayers and relics can have today. In a way, such topics are always relevant because they are both concerned with death, which comes to all. Prayer and friendship with the saints, who had passed through death, characterized Anselm's life from beginning to end, and there is a positive sense still that in using his words we are led into a clear space, into an age-long communion of souls linked together in a common service of love. The interiorization of prayer to which he gave such impetus has developed into a more personal, individual-centred spirituality, where all feel entitled to use their own words for themselves. The objective exercise of sharing the words and learning new ways of praying offered by Anselm can be clarifying and strengthening in this path of prayer, above all in preventing sheer boredom by the sense of refocused desire and channelled energy. In a culture where individuals are isolated and alone, the links with God and with others offered by prayer and friendship are increasingly valued, and through Anselm's prayers the idea of the community of heaven can be appreciated, enabling us to pass 'through the gate and grave of death' into a living experience of life here and now in the whole body of Christ.

While the way of prayer of Anselm is still relevant, this is not the case in most of northern Europe with relics. I am here talking about the secular world as well as Protestantism. The cult of relics is a more difficult topic for today, but there is perhaps something to be learned in seeing why this is so. Christian life throughout the thousand years which we call the Middle Ages involved relics; indeed it might to be said to have revolved round them, and the fact that this is not so now is a complex but revealing matter. The exception to this is of course the Roman Catholic and Orthodox Churches; this has been illustrated recently by the opening of Cardinal Newman's grave, with the intention of translating his remains to a place where they could be given due honour, and further clearing the way for his beatification.

In Anselm's day, not only churches and monasteries, monks, nuns, bishops and prelates but also kings, queens, merchants, soldiers and that almost invisible silent majority, the common people, sought to touch relics and if possible obtain them; they were essential for the consecration of a church, placed under or over the altar, displayed as the central part of a lord's treasure, made into glorious artefacts, exchanged in political deals, accepted as the spoils of war, stolen, given, worn on the person. If you asked any great lord between 500 and 1500 in what his wealth consisted, he would have listed first the content of his *hailigdom*, his relic collection. Today, there is no part of medieval life which is so opaque to most of us. I do not mean that we don't have relics or that souvenirs of the dead are no longer valued. Indeed we are more credulous than ever about that in certain ways: a friend of mine has a hair of Mozart; the tomb of Lenin in Red Square has all the elements of the veneration of the body of a saint about it; recently, I saw on sale in Oxford (for an absurd price) a small plastic tube said to contain the sweat of Marilyn Monroe. But these are not relics in the medieval sense. There has been a change of focus about reality and it has affected especially those relics which are bones. Books about relics treat bones as either macabre or as comic material, but that is to put our own assumptions upon alien ways of thought in a way which is as unwarranted as was the approach of Calvin and Herring. If we were to claim that we had in a bottle the last breath of St Joseph, I think we would do well to smile; we would certainly not put any money into its possession or risk our health and sanity on it. But our ideas are not those of the people who respected and valued such a relic. That is the result of many influences which have changed us; we are not necessarily better, just different. We may be sentimental about mementos, but we no longer put wealth into a collection of bones upon which we then rely. When thieves stole the bones of St Lucy some years ago from a church in Rome and demanded ransom money for their return, they were met with indifference and the bones of St Lucy, one the most revered saints of the early Church, were dumped in a rubbish bin. In England, the Orthodox Church began a court case to demand possession of the supposed bones of Edmund the Martyr for their own veneration; the judge said that he doubted whether anyone could possess the bones of another person, and the relics remain in a legal deed box. By and large, it is physical relics we don't care for and I think in trying to find out why, we can discover a lot about the Middle Ages and ourselves in general.

We have mementos, and in some places artefacts are treated as magical objects. Moreover, relics are not ignored today in the academic world. They are among the new sources, such as prayers, pilgrimages and miracles, which are seriously examined nowadays by historians of the Middle Ages. Bones and pieces of flesh or blood are not in themselves, of course, at all interesting to the historian: it is the reactions of people to them that provide a mine of information, social, economic, political, anthropological and psychological. This objective study of phenomena can also provide new insight into the religious world of the times.

The Middle Ages themselves criticized relics; we also have our criticism. It is precisely there, in the difference between their kind of criticism and ours, that it is possible to see the immense gap in understanding between ourselves and medieval people. As has been seen (Chapter 4, pp. 81–8) the moment when a new kind of criticism of relics emerged decisively was in the sixteenth century with the printing in 1543 of John Calvin's *Traite des Reliques*. Calvin criticized the cult of relics as being non-scriptural, idolatrous, and above all fraudulent; and to that he added the most destructive argument of all, that they were not and could not be what was claimed for them; he made it seem ridiculous to honour relics, and once ridicule has been suggested no one wants to be laughed at.

The first focus of the sixteenth-century Reformers, both Catholic and Protestant, in their searing criticism of relics, was the relics of Jesus Christ, and it is mainly those that I will now look at, as examples of the changes in attitude which lay behind the rejection of interest in the bones of saints such as those of Anselm. It is surprising in a theological sense to hear about relics of Jesus Christ: 'He is not here, he is risen' (Matt. 28.6). The fact of the resurrection of Christ from the dead is, in the Gospel, made real by the affirmation that no physical body remained in the tomb. His body was wholly taken into God, creating a new heaven and a new earth. I am not here under-taking an argument about the Gospel text but stating what was believed by the first two thousand years of Christian life and thought. Christ was risen and ascended and there could there-fore be no relics of Christ. But there were. The argument was that even if his crucified body had been wholly taken up into heaven, there were bits of his body that were not part of him at that moment. There were relics connected with the passion while Christ was dying but not yet dead: pieces of the cross,[1] nails, crown, thorns, scourge, spear, veil, sweat, blood, tears. There were also relics connected with his infancy and therefore with his mother (also one who, taken up into heaven bodily, left no relics behind her): there were pieces that came off before her death such as the umbilical cord of Jesus, his foreskin, milk teeth, and curls; there were also some hairs of the Virgin, her shift, her milk, her veil, her slipper. It seems to me that such relics were not well known before the eleventh century, with the exception of course of the relics of the true cross, which were talked about from the fourth century onwards They are perhaps connected with the major shift in focus in devotion which occurred at that time, from the veneration of the redeeming work of God in Christ to the identification with the man of sorrows. That is certainly one part of the background in considering the popularity of such relics and their multiplication through the ensuing centuries, as it was the origin for some strands in the prayers of Anselm. But having noted a connection between the thinking and praying of medieval people, perhaps it is possible to see, by looking at accounts of such relics, what they signified to those who used them. Let me take two only: blood and tears.

Two kinds of relics are meant by the phrase 'the blood of Christ'. First, the eucharistic remains of consecrated wine which became the blood of Christ; second, the blood from the wounds of Christ on the cross. Respect for an external manifestation of wine-become-blood at the Eucharist has a long history. The earliest story that I know of about the host and the eucharistic wine turning to actual blood and flesh at the moment of consecration is in the *Apophthegmata Patrum*, a collection made in the fourth century of stories and sayings connected with the first Christian monks in Egypt, and popular in its Latin version in the medieval Church and beyond. It is a story which sounds more like the thirteenth century than the fourth.

Abba Daniel quoted a story he had heard from Abba Arsenius about a monk who said that the body and blood of Christ in the Eucharist was a symbol only; he was shown during mass the bread which was placed upon the holy table as a little child. 'Then the priest put out his hand to break the bread, and behold an angel of the Lord came down from heaven with a knife in his hand and poured the child's blood into the chalice.'[2] This type of story was often repeated,[3] and by the twelfth century fragments of such flesh and blood were being regarded as relics, to be preserved, placed in shrines and venerated, even buried to consecrate the foundations of new churches. The holy blood of Hayles is one example, the blood at Bruges another. It was a story told to strengthen faith, propaganda for a specific view of the Eucharist. We would criticize it in that way; it also had its critics at the time, but for other reasons. In the twelfth century, that assiduous collector of relics of saints, the learned and saintly Carthusian, Hugh Bishop of Lincoln (see Chapter 4, p. 62), was never backward in obtaining and valuing relics of the saints. But when he stopped at the village of Joi on a journey from Paris to Troyes, where the parish priest invited him to see and venerate a chalice containing flesh and blood from the Eucharist to which 'large numbers of the faithful from the districts round come eagerly to see with their own eyes this wonderful work of God'. Hugh refused to see it, not because he doubted it, but because, he said,

> It is not our concern. Why should we gape at a sensory image of this divine gift when every day we behold by faith this heavenly sacrifice whole and entire? Let the man look with his bodily eyes who cannot by faith internally behold the whole.[4]

This was an approach Anselm would have agreed with, and in his prayer before the Eucharist his consideration was wholly biblical and personal, in no way concerned with relics.[5] Neither Hugh nor Anselm was expressing doubt about the theological reality of the sacrament, only about the appropriateness of preserving fragments. This was not the same at all as later denunciations, when the actual change was in itself denied, so that the Eucharist was regarded as a memorial service of a historical event, in which bread remained bread and wine wine, a very new way of thinking about reality.

The second kind of relic of the blood of Christ was blood which, it was claimed, had flowed from Christ's wounded hands and side on the cross before his death. This type of relic made a rather late appearance. It is a part of the growing intimate devotion to the passion of Christ which began with Anselm's prayer:

> Alas for me, that I was not able to see
> the Lord of Angels humbled to converse with men, . . .
> Why, O my soul, were you not there
> to be pierced by a sword of bitter sorrow
>   when you could not bear
> the piercing of the side of your Saviour with a lance? . . .
>   Why did you not see with horror
> The blood that poured out of the side of your Redeemer?[6]

It was a short step in devotion to imagining that you were present and could see the blood and could collect it. Visible remnants of it were forthcoming to focus this devotional need. Drops of blood were offered for veneration in Rome, at the churches of Santa Croce in Jerusalem, Santa Maria Maggiore and St John Lateran, and especially in Constantinople. The sack of that city in 1204 during the Fourth Crusade had caused an enormous number of relics to flow from Constantinople to the West, many of them connected with the passion of Christ. The chaplain of King Baldwin brought a phial of the blood of Christ to the abbey of St Jean-des-Vignes at Soissons, and the abbey of St Medard de Soissons claimed to have obtained from there one of the milk teeth of Jesus. Most notably, the crown of thorns formed the centre of the Sainte Chapelle, the glorious building which Pierre de Montreuil, the greatest contemporary architect of France, constructed for its reception in the centre of Paris on the orders of Louis IX of France. In 1204 Baldwin in Constantinople had been in urgent need of money to pay his troops for at least two years' service. He had therefore offered his brother Louis a deal: if he would pay his debts and finance the crusaders for a year, he would receive a package of supremely valuable and unique relics which included a fragment of the shroud, the reed, the lance and the crown of thorns. Two

Dominicans, Andrew and James, checked them and vouched for their authenticity. Such relics of Christ brought forth further criticism: the tooth at Soissons notoriously provoked Guibert of Nogent to protest, though not in terms of the modern theologian.[7]

No one seriously doubted that such relics were pre-eminent ways to contact heaven: it was not doubt that they aroused but envy. The appearance of a phial of the blood of Christ in England was in some part a national answer to the French reliquary of Louis IX. In 1247–48 Matthew Paris recorded an event which he says he witnessed and was asked to write about by the King Henry III: 'the coming of the Holy Blood to England. Oct 13th 1247'.[8] There was a triple celebration in Westminster: to honour the translation of the body of King Edward the Martyr; for the knighting of the king's half-brother William of Valence, but the first reason given in the King's summons to his magnates was 'most agreeable news of a holy benefit recently conferred by God on the English'. Its exact nature was kept secret perhaps in order to make sure everyone would come out of curiosity. The new relic was vouched for by outstandingly reputable people: the masters of the Templars and Hospitallers with the testimony of good reputable people, namely the patriarch of Jerusalem, and other archbishops and bishops, abbots and other prelates and magnates of the Holy Land. It was claimed that they had sent some of the blood of our Lord which he shed on the cross for the salvation of the world, in a most beautiful crystal container, in the care of a certain well-known brother of the Knights Templar. The relic was solemnly received by Henry III who took personal charge of it:

> The king the pious Henry fasted and kept vigil all night then in the morning took the container in solomn procession from St Pauls to Westminster Abbey, where he carried it all round the church and his own apartments, then gave it to St Peter at Westminster.

The Bishop of Norwich, Walter Suffield, preached a sermon at mass in Westminster Abbey that day, commending the relic in somewhat political not to say nationalistic terms: this blood was, he said, 'of all things most sacred among men because it was shed for the salvation of all; it was more sacred than the cross which was only sacred because of the blood on it'. Therefore this relic, he suggested, was more holy than that owned by the King of France; it would give great blessings to England; and it was given into the keeping of the English because their King was a saint and it was suitably brought from Syria, which was desolate because 'faith and holiness flourish more here than in any part of the world'.

An indulgence of six years and 116 days was offered to all who venerated it. Reassurance about the relic first rested on the classic proof of the testimony of good men: Thierry, the lay prior of the Hospitallers in Jerusalem, reassured them by saying, first, that there had been no bribes or exchange of money in this and, second, why should those giving it perjure their souls by lying about it? The preacher appealed to a sense of rivalry about its ownership, a nationalistic one-upmanship, adding the statement that in its original place in Syria it had not been worthily venerated and therefore ought to be transferred to a place more ready to honour it, a common argument for the translation of relics. The practical bribe of a lavish indulgence concluded the defence of this relic from any possible critic. But there was still a theological criticism to be met: how could the Lord have left his blood upon earth when he arose again full and entire in body the third day after his resurrection? This question was dealt with by Thomas Aquinas, whose answer was that all parts of the Lord's body must have risen at his resurrection and therefore nothing could remain – an answer not helpful to the relic in question, and therefore the preacher quoted instead Robert Grosseteste of Lincoln, who held that such remnants, left behind before death, could exist.

A similar relic of Christ was his tears. Tears have always had a great deal of significance in Christian devotion. They signify the waters of baptism, the coming of the Spirit over the waters of creation and re-creation, that breaking open and moving of the stone upon the heart so that waters of cleansing and re-birth can gush out. The history of Christian understanding of *compunctio cordis* has this as its central element: to weep was necessary for any saint or man of prayer. Arsenius in the desert wept so much that his tears carved channels down his face.[9] Anselm wrote about them in several of his prayers, and his biographer saw weeping as one of the signs of Anselm's own sanctity. In many ways the eleventh century was especially a century of this kind of tears. The tears wept by Christ over Jerusalem on his way to the cross therefore attracted particular attention, as did the tears shed when he wept for Lazarus: the words 'Jesus wept' and his lament 'O Jerusalem, Jerusalem' were particularly evocative of the grief of the man of sorrows. Prayer focused on such tears with interior emotion and it was not long before phials containing relics of these tears were shown at several places in northern France: at St Maximin-la-sainte-Baume in Provence, the supposed tomb of Lazarus, the church of St Leonard in Anjou, the cathedral at Marsilles, the abbey of Fontcarmont, St Pierre le Puellier in Orleans, the church of the Holy Trinity in Vendome, and especially at the abbey of St Peter at Selincourt. In 1206 the Emperor Henry had suceeded Baldwin and like him was in dire need of money for his troops. He rewarded his main military leaders, whom he could not pay, with such relics, and it says much for the value of relics that tough old soldiers should have accepted them. Bernard, lord of Marevil in Provence, accepted for two years' campaigning a crystal phial containing a tear of Christ. He left for home at once and built a chapel for it in his castle, where it formed the centre of his relic collection, the envy of his neighbours. There was protest, not for historical and theological reasons, but because the local church considered that such a major relic should not be in private and secular hands. Finally, Bernard met their protests three years later by giving it to the new Praemonstratensian abbey of St Peter at Selincourt where his uncle was the abbot.[10]

Anselm was not deeply concerned with such tangible relics of Christ, but it was his new type of devotion that had caused this kind of interest. It was a short step for many from Anselm's

> Would that I with happy Joseph
> might have taken down my Lord from the cross

in his *Prayer to Christ*, to the Middle English *A Talking of the Love of God* (of which a large part was based directly on Anselm's prayers) with its 'I leap upon him as a greyhound at an hart; I fold him in my arms; I suck the blood from his feet.' This style of emotion was often connected with relics of Christ's blood, cross and tears, and did in fact lead to master-pieces of devotion such as the *Stabat mater dolorosa* or indeed the treasure of Protestant hymnody, 'When I survey the won-drous cross'. But this was a development from the imaginative personal involvement Anselm initiated, which had always been firmly based on Scripture and made use of emotion only as a trigger to charity and discipleship.

Another result of emotive concentration on the details of Christ's passion in relation to relics was equally far from Anselm's mind. The relics of Christ were, like other relics of saints, subject to manipulation and politics. The new eleventh-century devotion was the mainspring for their increased value, and the more cynical and materialistic aspects in no way destroyed the respect and veneration offered to them. The emphasis was on what was interior, what the holiness behind the relic could do practically for the individual or the group here and now; validity and historicity played no part in the matter. Relics connected with the passion were used in financial deals, in military strategies, in political alliances. There were instances even where the force of local and popular devotion to a holy one's bones overrode any theological framework and indeed appalled the theologically sophisticated. Perhaps the most extreme instance of this is the martyr-cult of St Guinefort in the village of Dombes, forty kilometres north of Lyons in the middle of the thirteenth century. The Dominican preacher Stephen of Bourbon described in his collection of stories for the use of preachers how he had visited Dombes some years earlier and had heard reports there of a healing shrine especially efficacious for sick children. He inquired into the life and times of this saint, in accordance with the new demands of the process of canonization set up in 1214: what outstanding signs of charity had been manifested in this life for the approval of man as well as the signs of the approval of God in miracles? The story was all that could be desired: a babysitter for the baby boy of the lord and lady of a castle near Neuville had saved a child from death when a serpent had entered the house in their absence by killing it and in the process being covered with blood. On their return the parents saw a disarranged and blood-covered cradle, a babysitter also stained with blood, and at once the father thought the babysitter was to blame. He drew his sword and killed the murderer of the child; he then found the baby alive and untouched, with the dead body of the snake under the cradle. A martyr, innocently slain, who had died out of love for a child; no wonder the villagers buried him with respect and were convinced that he would care still about babies. And indeed many women told Stephen that their children had been cured at that grave: what concerned the villagers was that the relics worked and cured their children. The only problem for the friar was that 'St Guinefort' had been a greyhound. He was scandalized and ordered the bones of the dog to be taken out and scattered. The legend of the babysitter animal who kills a predator and then is slain by the parents who see only blood and no baby is very old indeed: a version is found in Sanskrit literature in the sixth century BC. A deeply meaningful story for centuries, and who is to say it did not from time

to time happen? The people of Dombes knew only one thing:
their children were cured by this holy one; when the friar left,
they collected the bones and reburied them. The last mention
of this shrine is in the mid nineteenth century.[11]

There was, then, criticism of relics throughout the Middle
Ages in various ways, as well as an astute attitude to their value.
People were after all well able to hold more than one idea in
their minds at once and see no hypocrisy in doing so. But with
the sixteenth century, a new note sounded, a new mental
approach which made impossible the cult of relics, and especially those of Jesus Christ. This came from a theological out-
look on the world very different from that of Anselm. Relics,
the new critics said, were not mentioned in the Bible, or not
connected with evangelical holiness; it was impossible to see
historical continuity about the existence of most of them and
they therefore must be frauds; even if genuine, they were idols,
coming between the people and God. Questions about how,
mechanics, time and place and historicity took the place of
questions of why, and what did they do for personal devotion
and spiritual profit. Such differences of attitude continue and
make it hard for us to enter into the earlier love of relics, without seeming simple-minded, yet they were venerated by serious
and highly intelligent people, whose ideas in other areas we
take seriously.

The cult of saints and their relics shows some things that
separate us from the age of Anselm, perhaps not altogether to
our advantage. There is clearly a different approach to reality,
different questions about evidence: the question of the early
ages was 'What will it do for us, spiritually or materially, now?'
not 'How did it get here?' But accepting that, what can we see in
these records that is neither better nor worse but simply quite
different? There are three areas in which change has taken
place.

The first thing that has changed between Anselm and today
is the ability to see the whole within a small part: it is no

coincidence that the change in approach to relics comes at the same time as a change in thinking about the Eucharist. In his prayer before receiving Communion, Anselm wrote, 'I thank you for the good gift of this your holy Body and Blood', seeing Christ within the sacrament. At the Reformation this ability to see the whole Christ in the host was replaced by a commemoration of a historical event, the last supper of Jesus with his disciples. At the same time, the ability to see the whole gospel in any word of the Scriptures was replaced by the historical hunt for the meaning of its authors. A king was no longer his whole nation. In the same way, a small piece of bone was no longer the whole presence and power of the saint standing before Christ. The bones of those whom people knew to have been filled with the Spirit, who had been seen by their charity to have put on Christ, had been held to have some traces of heavenly fragrance still within them. They even smelled of heaven, as Eadmer says Anselm's bones did, and they would rise at the last day. Meanwhile where they rested there was a guaranteed private line to heaven. After the sixteenth century bones became fragments from the past whose provenance in time had to be established. The production of portraits, physical descriptions, in the end photographs, gradually replaced this sense of the continued presence of the dead in any fragment connected with the saints, by a dead historical record of them in their earthly life.

Second, there is for us a privatization of death and bones. For the early Church and for the Middle Ages the apprehension of death as a glorious moment of passing over from death into life caused it to be public and central: no one lived, begot or died alone. Anselm died in public among the monks of Canterbury and other visitors, speculating about the state of the soul, and his body was treated with the greatest care and reverence. The seventeenth century had a quite different interest in bones, death, decay and skeletons. Webster was 'much possessed with death and saw the skull beneath the skin' (T. S.

Eliot). John Donne, though he also understood in his sermons
the gate of death as a portal into life, wrote more satirically of
bones, relics and burial:

> When my grave is broke up again,
> Some second guest to entertain . . .
> And he that digs it, spies
> A bracelet of bright hair about the bone . . .
> If this fall in a time, or land,
> Where mis-devotion doth command,
> Then, he that digs us up, will bring
> Us, to the Bishop, and the King,
> To make us relics; then
> Thou shalt be a Mary Magdalen, and I
> A something else thereby.
> > 'The Relique'

The disturbing of bones is a 'mis-devotion' to Donne, leading
to idolatry, and those who have died will not meet again until
'at that last busie day' when they 'meet at this grave and make a
little stay'.

That sense of the skeleton, the horror of the bone and the
flesh, as separation and isolation, was not how medieval
people, including Anselm, saw death and dissolution. For them,
the body was transparent with glory, more and more so in
weakness and death: as with the Scriptures, so with the body,
they could say, 'Blessed are the eyes that see divine spirit
through the letter's veil'.

Third, there is a change in our attitude to the body and belief
in the resurrection of the body and the communion of the
saints. The final clauses of the creed were interpreted as immediate and not future only: heaven and the saints were alive and
available here and now. For Anselm, life given by God connected
all members of the body of Christ living and dead, and that was
a life which connects humankind also with all creation. The
communion of saints existed: those still alive lived in the sixth
age which was always paralleled by the seventh age of the saints,

both ending in the eighth day of the Lord. There was a sense that the body does not divide us into individual units which cannot communicate, cannot love or be loved, and which will fall apart at death. Today we are isolated from each other as well as from the dead:

> Some thirty inches from my nose
> The frontier of my person goes,
> And all the untilled air between
> Is private pagus or demesne.
> Stranger, unless with bedroom eyes
> I beckon you to fraternize
> Beware of rashly crossing it:
> I have no gun but I can spit.
>   (W. H. Auden, from 'Thanksgiving for a Habitat')[12]

The message of the cult of relics and prayer to the saints such as that of Anselm is surely that we are not just alive in our minds but in all our selves, and that the self does not need to make this terrified or self-indulgent choice of staying isolated and incapable of contact. Here and now is the place of God, where we are compassed about by a great cloud of witnesses, of dead friends who are not less but more alive.

When approaching any part of the past some spark of imagination is nececessary for us to begin to make both saints and their relics live, and this is true surely of our interest in anything in the past at all. The historical novel, the film, the song or the poem, perhaps *Monty Python and the Holy Grail*, have done more for us than any history book in alerting us to the past. But once we have decided to take that journey into the past, we need to put away our modern baggage and go there naked. The past has to speak for itself, in its own terms, before we can put to it the interests we have today. Only by seeing and respecting the attitudes and assumptions of the past can it be understood: we 'stand under' in order to 'understand'. So with Anselm's prayers and relics, both offer a vast field of material which is hard to handle, but immensely rewarding.

There have been from the sixteenth to the end of the twentieth century very deep and many-sided changes in thinking which have affected the attitudes to prayers to the saints, relics and death. At first sight it seems that nothing so underlines the gulf between ourselves and the Middle Ages as the cult of relics and the cult of the saints. But the records of that cult ought to be taken seriously on the terms of those who used them, and to do so is to discover insight into a whole world. It is not one which I find I can in any way patronize or ignore. There is truth in the history of the cult of the saints which it is important to recognize and respect; and in discovering this, we are brought face to face with the fact that knowledge is not, as we suppose technology to be, getting more and more effective: other cultures in the present and other eras in the past have had quite different ways of thinking about reality, no less effective, perhaps more so. Charles Jones, in his wonderful book, *St Nicholas of Myra, Bari and Manhattan*, deplores the modern attitude which dismisses a saint for the crime of never having existed and concludes: 'There is a reality in images, a life and perhaps a death, lacking in the truth of propositions.' Or, as Solzhenitsyn put it in his Nobel prize essay, *One Word of Truth*: 'Not everything has a name. Some things lead us into a realm beyond words. Art thaws even the frozen darkened soul, opening it to lofty spiritual experience. Through art we are sometimes sent indistinctly, briefly, revelations not to be achieved by rational thought.'[13]

The cult of the saints includes for us Anselm, both in his love of the saints, his discreet distancing from relics and as himself a saint. There is a consistency about Anselm from childhood to his death and beyond. A mind always alert and questioning in order to know better what was already believed, whether it was as a child in dialogue with God at the top of a mountain, or at the age of seventy-six on his deathbed at Canterbury, wondering if he would have time to elucidate the origin of the soul more clearly for the sake of others, since 'I do not know who will do this after I am dead'. In this he was like Bede, who worked on the Gospel of John to his last moment, for the love of learning in the service of others, held within the constant desire for God. For them scholarship was a way of life to be continued every day and in every circumstance. Neither monk was anxious about death, nor wanting to extend life for its own sake. They were both realistic about themselves as used by God and they were both always ready for anything God wanted of them, without sentimentality and also without fear. Anselm in particular, with his intense sense of his own creatureliness and lack of goodness, provides a unique illustration of the fact that the Christian saint is no remote superman. The words and deeds of human beings are gradually and entirely filled and transfigured by the presence of God in Christ who is reconciling, secretly, mysteriously, the world to himself. Anselm is not remembered only as wise, great or righteous, but as a humble and sinful human being, loved by some, disliked by others, who, through who knows what agonies and darknesses, had so learned to walk in faith in Christ in daily life that at the moment of death he revealed to others, if not to himself, that underneath are the everlasting arms that hold us. The connecting point in examining Anselm's prayers to the saints and the relics of saints and of himself is to see this quiet connection between life and death: the end of physical, fleshly life being the way into the real life of heaven. In this the relics, as remnants of flesh once imbued with divinity, had a place, and provided a point to realize that the prayers of the saints they had belonged to were alive for the present care of those still living in the flesh. This marked out an immediate end here and now to death as 'the last enemy'. Anselm's relics are discreetly hidden: his prayers are gloriously alive. It seems right to address him as a saint among saints.

In the twelfth canto of the *Paradiso*, Dante arranged the saints in two concentric circles with:

all the singing, all the gleaming flames . . .
a loving jubilee of light with light.[14]

Dante placed Anselm there among the twelve saints in the outer circle of dancing lights around Dante and Beatrice, between John Chrysostom and Donatus, the Greek theologian and the Latin grammarian and opposite the Spanish scholar, Isidore of Seville.

> Hugh of St Victor is among them . . .
> And the patriarch Chrysostom, Anselm, and Donatus
> . . . with dancing and sublime festivity.[15]

This is the final place to see Anselm, dancing among the stars which are the saints, entirely himself, and entirely part of the whole circle of the redeemed, a scholar among scholars, yet finally held with them by what had always been the end of his desire, 'the love that moves the sun and the other stars'.[16]

Notes

Short titles of translations of works by Anselm and his biographer Eadmer, as used in these notes. For full bibliographical details see Bibliography.

Letters refers to *Letters of St Anselm*, trans. Walter Frohlich.
Prayers, Meditations, Proslogion refer to *Prayers and Meditations of St Anselm*, trans. Benedicta Ward.
Life refers to *The Life of St Anselm* by Eadmer, trans. R. W. Southern.
History refers to *Eadmer's History of Recent Events in England*, trans. G. Bosanquet.

1 Who was Anselm?

1 *Life*, 1.1, p. 3.
2 Anselm, Letter 211, *Letters*, Vol. 2, p. 159.
3 R. W. Southern and F. S. Schmitt (eds), *Memorials of St Anselm* (Oxford, 1969).
4 *Life*, 2.66, p. 141.
5 *Life*, 2.66, pp. 141–3.
6 William Stubbs, *Historical Introductions to the Rolls Series* (London, 1902), p. 112.
7 E. B. Pusey, *Meditations and Prayers to the Holy Trinity and Our Lord Jesus Christ* (Oxford, 1856).
8 For a recent discussion of the prayers later associated with Anselm, see Jean-François Cottier, *Anima mea: prières privées et textes de dévotion du Moyen Age latin* (Turnout, Brepols, 2002).
9 *Memorials of St Anselm*, ed. R. W. Southern and F. S. Schmitt (London, 1969), p. 2.
10 *Meditation on Human Redemption*, pp. 230–7, at 237. Cf. discussion of the *Prayers and Meditations* in R. W. Southern, *St Anselm: A Portrait in a Landscape* (Cambridge, 1990), pp. 91–134; also discussed in *Les Méditations et Prières de S. Anselme*, French trans. D. A. Castel (Paris, 1923), introduction by André Wilmart.

11 *Proslogion,* pp. 238–67.

12 *Life,* 2.72, pp. 150–1.

13 *History,* pp. 111–12.

14 William of Malmesbury, *Gesta Pontificum Anglorum,* Vol. 1 Latin text ed. and trans. M. Winterbottom (Oxford, 2007), Bk 1.65, p. 195.

2 Anselm, friend of sinners: the penitent's desire for heaven

1 *Life,* 2.71, p. 149.

2 *Life,* 1.5, p. 9.

3 *Meditation 2,* pp. 225–8.

4 R. Drake, *A Manual of the Private Devotions and Meditations of Lancelot Andrewes* (London, 1648), preface, p. 4.

5 Anselm, *Why God Became Man,* section 2, p. 306.

6 *Why God Became Man,* section 2, p. 308.

7 *Meditation 1,* p. 221.

8 *Prayer to St Nicholas,* p. 184, lines 14–15.

9 *Prayer to St John Evangelist (1),* p. 158, lines 43 and 35.

10 *Prayer to St Nicholas,* p. 192, lines 250–1.

11 E. B. Pusey, *Meditations and Prayers to the Holy Trinity and Our Lord Jesus Christ* (Innes and Co, 1856), p. 31.

12 *Meditation 2,* p. 226.

13 *Meditation 1,* p. 221.

14 Day of wrath, O day of mourning!
See fulfilled the prophet's warning,
Heaven and earth in ashes burning.
Oh, what fear man's bosom rendeth
When from Heav'n the Judge descendeth
On Whose sentence all dependeth!
    'Dies irae dies illa', Thomas of Celano, trans. William J. Irons, 1848. See, e.g., *Hymns Ancient and Modern* (1924), No. 398, p. 339.

15 Letter to Gunhilda, *Letters,* Vol. 2, Letter 168, p. 64.

16 Letter to Gunhilda, *Letters,* Vol. 2, Letter 169, p. 72.

17 Letter about Mathilda to Osmund of Salisbury, *Letters,* Vol. 2, Letter 117, pp. 91–2.

18 Letter from Mathilda, *Letters,* Vol. 2, Letter 242, p. 221. In spite of the overwhelming flattery of this and several other letters from

the queen to Anselm, his early expressions of affection for her faded; he was nowhere as warm towards her as to Gunhilda or Frodelinda.

19 For Eadmer's account of the problems involved in Mathilda's marriage, cf. *History*, pp. 136–41.

20 *Meditation 1*, p. 224.

21 *Meditation on Human Redemption*, p. 237; *Prayer before Receiving the Body and Blood of Christ*, p. 101; *Proslogion*, pp. 264 and 265.

22 Jeremy Taylor, *The Life of our Blessed Lord and Saviour Jesus Christ the Great Exemplar of Sanctity and Holy Life*, in *The Whole Works* ed. Reginald Heber, rev. Charles Page Eden (London, 1847), Vol. 2, p. 514.

23 *Meditation on Human Redemption*, p. 235.

24 Cf. R. W. Southern, *The Making of the Middle Ages* (London, 1953), Ch. 5, 'From epic to romance', pp. 209–44.

25 *Prayer to St Mary (2)*, pp. 112–13.

26 *Life*, p. 163.

27 R. W. Southern, *Anselm and His Biographer* (Cambridge, 1963), p. 42.

28 *Life*, 1.7, p. 12.

29 D. Knowles, *Saints and Scholars: Twenty-Five Medieval Portraits* (Cambridge, 1961), p. 32.

30 Cf. Southern, *Anselm and His Biographer*, Ch. V, pp. 194–226, for further discussion of Ralph, Eadmer, Baldwin, Alexander, Eustace and Gilbert Crispin.

31 *Life*, 2.8, p. 70.

32 *Life*, 2.31, p. 107.

33 *Life*, 2.30, p. 107.

34 *Life*, 1.7, p. 12.

35 *Life*, 2.59, p. 136.

36 *Prayer for Friends*, p. 213.

37 *Life*, 2.33, p. 111.

38 *Life*, 1.10, p. 17.

39 *Life*, 1.10, p. 20.

40 *Life*, 1.20, Letter to Lanzo, pp. 32–4.

41 *Prayer to St Benedict*, pp. 196–200, at p. 198.

42 *Life*, 1.19, p. 30.

43 Preface to *Prayers and Meditations*, p. 89.

44 Letter 112 to Hugh the Hermit, *Letters*, Vol. 1, pp. 268–70.

45 Letter 45 to Frodelinda, *Letters*, Vol. 1, pp. 151–2.
46 Athanasius, *Life of St Anthony the Great*, trans. Robert Meyer (London, 1950), cap. 20, p. 37.

3 Anselm, friend of the saints

1 *Life*, 2.24, pp. 99–100.
2 *Life*, p. 100.
3 *Life*, 2.26, p. 106.
4 *Life*, 2.29, p. 105.
5 *Life*, 1.8, p. 14.
6 Cf. the *Life of St Bernard*, 6, in *PL* 185, cols. 469–524.
7 *Life*, 1.2, pp. 4–5.
8 *Proslogion*, 26, p. 266.
9 *Prayer to St John the Baptist*, p. 128.
10 *Life*, 2.65, p. 141.
11 *Prayer Before Receiving the Body and Blood of Christ*, p. 101.
12 *Proslogion*, 1, p. 239.
13 Letter 112 to Hugh the Hermit, *Letters*, Vol. 1, p. 268.
14 *Life*, 1.6, p. 10.
15 For an introduction to the new Orders see Bede Lackner, *The Eleventh Century Background to Citeaux* (Kalamazoo, 1976).
16 *Proslogion*, 1, p. 239.
17 *Proslogion*, 25, p. 263.
18 Origen, *Homilia in Genesim*, ed. Louis Doutreleau, Sources Chretiénnes 7 (Paris, 1976), 6.1; cf. Beryl Smalley, *The Study of the Bible in the Middle Ages* (Oxford, 1941).
19 Claudius of Turin, *Sermon on Leviticus*, *PL* 104, cols 615–17.
20 Bede, *On Genesis*, ed. J. A. Giles (London, 1843), ch. 14, pp. 173–4.
21 Bede, 'On the Dedication of a Church' Homily 2.25 in *The Venerable Bede: Homilies on the Gospels*, Book 2, trans. David Hurst and Lawrence Martin (Kalamazoo, 1991), p. 267.
22 For Augustine/Bede on the ages of man, cf. J. A. Burrow, *The Ages of Man* (Oxford, 1986).
23 Cf. my 1991 Jarrow Lecture, *Bede and the Psalter* (reprinted SLG, Oxford, 1992).
24 *Prayers and Meditations*, Letter to Adelaide, pp. 172–3.
25 Cf. my Introduction to *Prayers and Meditations*, pp. 35–50.
26 *Meditation 1*, p. 224.

27 *Prayer to Christ*, pp. 95, 96.

28 *Prayers and Meditations*, Letter to Gundolf, p. 106.

29 Cf. A. Wilmart, 'Les propres corrections de S. Anselme dans sa grande prière a la Vierge Marie', *Revue de théologie ancienne et médiévale* 11 (1930), pp. 189–204.

30 *Life*, 1.8, pp. 14–15.

31 *Prayer to St Mary (3)*, p. 120.

32 *Life*, 2.32, p. 110.

33 *Prayer to St John the Baptist*, p. 127.

34 *Prayer to St Peter*, p. 137.

35 *Prayer to St Paul*, p. 152.

36 *Prayers to St John the Evangelist*, pp. 157–62; 163–76.

37 *Prayer to St Mary Magdalene*, p. 201.

38 Cf. Benedicte Ward, *Harlots of the Desert: A Study of Repentance in Early Monastic Sources* (Kalamazoo, 1987), ch. 1, 'Mary Magdalene'.

39 *Prayer to St Mary Magdalene*, p. 202.

40 Letter to the Princess Adelaide, *Prayers and Meditations*, pp. 172–3.

41 *Prayer to St Stephen*, p. 174.

42 Letter to Prior Baldric and the other Brethren at Bec, *Prayers and Meditations*, p. 183.

43 *Prayer to St Nicholas*, pp. 184, 186, 194.

44 *Prayer to St Benedict*, p. 196.

45 *Prayer by a Bishop or Abbot to the Patron Saint of his Church*, p. 208.

46 *Prayer by a Bishop or Abbot*; I have discussed this prayer in detail in a forthcoming book of essays on Anselm to be published in the USA.

47 Augustine, Sermon 340, *PL* 38, cols 280–2.

4 Anselm and the veneration of relics

1 *Letter of Polycarp to the Philippians*, in *The Apostolic Fathers*, Gk text and Eng. trans. Kirsopp Lake (London, 1919), p. 283.

2 *Martyrdom of St Polycarp*, trans. H. Musurillo *The Acts of the Christian Martyrs* (Oxford, 1972), pp. 3–21.

3 *Martyrdom of St Polycarp*, p. 19.

4 *Epistles of St Ignatius of Antioch* in *The Apostolic Fathers*, Gk text and Eng. trans. Kirsopp Lake (London, 1919), iv, p. 231.

5 Jerome *Contra Vigilantium*, PL 23, col. 404.

6 Paulinus, *Letter xxxi to Severus*, PL 19, cols 349–51.

7 Augustine, *City of God*, trans. Henry Bettenson (Harmondsworth, 1972), Book 22, pp. 1046–7.

8 Cyril of Jerusalem, *Catechetical Lectures*, 18.16.

9 Augustine, Sermon 317, PL 38, cols 280–2.

10 Jerome, *Contra Vigilantium*, col. 4.

11 Ephraim the Syrian, *Selected Works of S. Ephraim the Syrian*, trans. J. B. Morris (Oxford, 1847), p. 229, note a, Vol. 2.

12 Gregory of Tours, *The Glory of the Martyrs*, trans. R. Van Dam (Liverpool, 1983).

13 Eddius Stephanus, *The Life of Bishop Wilfrid*, ed. and trans. Bertram Colgrave (Cambridge, 1927), ch. 33, p. 67.

14 *Life of Bishop Wilfrid*, ch. 34, p. 71.

15 Gregory of Tours, *History of the Franks*, trans. Lewis Thorpe, Penguin Classics (Harmondsworth, 1974), p. 13.

16 Cf. Patrick J. Geary, *Furta Sacra: The Theft of Relics in the Central Middle Ages* (Princeton, 1978).

17 *Vita Sancti Malachiae, Opera Omnia S. Bernardi*, ed. J. Leclercq, C. H. Talbot and H. M. Rochais, 8 vols (Rome, 1957–78), Vol. 3, p. 308.

18 *Life*, 2.30, p. 51.

19 *Life*, 2.30, p. 53.

20 Letter 39, *Letters*, Vol. 1, pp. 139–40.

21 Letter 236, *Letters*, Vol. 2, pp. 212–13.

22 Letter 237, *Letters*, Vol. 2, pp. 213–14.

23 *History*, p. 143.

24 Letter 473, *Letters*, Vol. 3, pp. 266–7.

25 Asser, *Life of Alfred*, trans. R. Sharp, Penguin Classics (Harmondsworth, 1983), Appendix 1, 'Alfred and the Cakes', pp. 198–202 and note 142, pp. 254–5.

26 Adam of Eynsham, *Life of St Hugh of Lincoln*, ed. and trans. D. L. Douai and H. Farmer, 2 vols (London, 1962–63), Vol. 2, p. 167.

27 Adam, *Life of St Hugh*, pp. 169–70.

28 Adam, *Life of St Hugh*, pp. 28, 170–1.

29 Adam, *Life of St Hugh*, p. 167.

30 *History*, pp. 192–4.

31 Ordericus Vitalis (1075–c. 1142), *Ecclesiastical History*, 6 vols, ed. and trans. M. Chibnall (Oxford, 1969–80), Vol. 3, p. 171.

32 Eadmer, *History*, p. 193.
33 2 Tim. 4.19: 'Salute Prisca and Aquila'; Rom. 16.3: 'Greet Prisca and Aquila'; 1 Cor. 16.19: 'Aquila and Prisca salute you'; Acts 18.2: 'A certain Jew named Aquila . . . with his wife Priscilla', and cf. Acts 18.18 and 26. The identification of 'Prisca' with 'Priscilla' is not at all certain.
34 *Life*, 2.54, pp. 132–4.
35 *History*, p. 173.
36 *Life*, pp. 133–4.
37 Cf. C. W. Jones, *Saint Nicholas of Myra, Bari, and Manhattan: Biography of a Legend* (Chicago and London, 1978).
38 *Prayer to St Nicholas*, pp. 185, 194–5.
39 *The 'Vita Wulfstani' of William of Malmesbury*, ed. and trans. R. R. Darlinton, Camden Society Series 3, Vol. 40 (London, 1928), pp. 42–3.

5 Canonization: *Doctor Magnificus*

1 Prosper Lambertini (later Benedict XIV), *De Servorum Dei Beatificatione et Beatorum Canonizatione* (Bologna, 1734–38).
2 E. W. Kemp, *Canonization and Authority in the Western Church* (Oxford, 1948).
3 *Decreta authentica congregationis sacrorum rituum sub auspices Leonis papae XIII* (Rome, 1888), 5 vols.
4 For this grant and for other documents concerning Anselm's posthumous reputation at Canterbury see W. Urry, 'St Anselm and his Cult at Canterbury' in *Spicilegium Beccense* 1 (Paris, 1959), pp. 571–93.
5 *Life*, 2.66, pp. 142–3.
6 William of Malmesbury, *Gesta Pontificum Anglorum*, ed. and trans. R. M. Thomson and M. Winterbottom, Vols 1 and 2 (Oxford, 2007).
7 MS Bodley C 260 fol. 2v; cf. R. W. Southern, *Anselm and His Biographer* (Cambridge, 1963), p. 339.
8 Gervase of Canterbury, *De Combustibus*: cf. C. E. Woodruff and W. Danks, *Memorials of the Cathedral and Priory of Christ in Canterbury* (London, 1912), ch. 5, 'The Great Fire', pp. 89–102.
9 'List of Prior Eastry', in J. W. Legg and W. H. St J. Hope, *Inventories of Christ Church* (London, 1905), p. 111.

10 Cf. A. Saltman, *Theobald, Archbishop of Canterbury* (London, 1995), pp. 241ff.

11 *The Eadwine Psalter: Text, Image and Monastic Culture in Twelfth-Century Canterbury*, ed. M. Gibson, T. A. Heslop and R. W. Pfaff (Pennsylvania, 1992), pp. 64ff, 'The Calendar'.

12 Letter of Alexander III to Thomas Becket, in *The Letters of Thomas Becket Archbishop of Canterbury, 1162–1170*, ed. and trans. Anne Duggan (Oxford, 2000), Vol. 1, Letter 10, pp. 27–8.

13 See note 7 above.

14 W. Urry, 'St Anselm'.

15 Urry, 'St Anselm'.

16 R. W. Southern, *Anselm and His Biographer*, p. 342.

17 Clementis XI, *Opera Omnia* (Frankfurt, 1729), col. 1215.

6 Anselm's relics

1 Augustine, *On the Work of Monks*, trans. H. Browne, Nicene and Post-Nicene Fathers, First Series, Vol. 3, ed. Philip Schaff (Buffalo, NY, 1887), ch. 36.

2 Guibert of Nogent, *De Pignoribus Sanctis*, PL 156, col. 608.

3 *Materials for the History of Thomas Becket Archbishop of Canterbury*, 7 vols, ed. J. C. Robinson, Rolls Series (London, 1875–85), Vol. 4, p. 216.

4 For Luther on relics, cf. The 95 Theses (1517).

5 Erasmus, *A Pilgrimage for Religion's Sake* in *Collected Works of Erasmus, Vol. 40*, ed. and trans. C. R. Thompson (Toronto, 1997).

6 Calvin, *Traite des reliques* (1543): see J. Calvin, *Treatise on Relics*, trans. and introd. V. Krasinski (Edinburgh, 1854).

7 Luther, *Table Talk*.

8 The second Royal Injunctions of Henry VIII 1538, in *English Historical Documents Vol. 5 (1485–1558)*, ed. C. W. Williams (London, 1967).

9 John Blair, *St Frideswide of Oxford* (Oxford, 1989), pp. 21–2.

10 Letters of Thomas Herring.

11 Letter of Archbishop Herring to the Dean of Canterbury: these letters are all found in the archives of Canterbury Cathedral.

12 In the last letter, 'Lord Bolton' as a title seems to have been disused by this time, but 'Bolton' might refer to Charles Ingoldsby Paulet, 13th Marquess of Winchester (1765–1843). It

may not be correct, however, to attribute the letter by this name anyway: 'Bolton' itself may not be right, since the signature is badly written.

13 For an excellent discussion of Anselm's reputation in the ninteenth century, see G. E. M. Gasper, 'An Anglican Anselm', in *Anselm and Abelard: Investigations and Juxtapositions*, ed. G. E. M. Gasper and H. Kohlenberger (Toronto, 2006), pp. 103–17.

7 Anselm today

1 For a modern discussion of the relics of the true cross, cf. Stephan Borgehammar, *How the Holy Cross Was Found* (Stockholm, 1991).

2 *The Desert Fathers: Sayings of the Early Christian Monks*, ed. and trans. Benedicta Ward (London, 2003), Section 18.3, pp. 185–6.

3 Cf. Miri Rubens, *Corpus Christi: The Eucharist in Late Medieval Culture* (Cambridge, 1991), pp. 135–9.

4 Adam of Eynsham, *Life of St Hugh of Lincoln*, ed. and trans. D. L. Douai and H. Farmer (London, 1962–63), Vol. 2, p. 168.

5 *Prayer Before Receiving the Body and Blood of Christ*, pp. 100–1.

6 *Prayer to Christ*, p. 97. A recent discussion of the relics of the holy blood can be found in Caroline Bynum, *Wonderful Blood* (Philadelphia, 2007).

7 Guibert of Nogent, *De Pignoribus Sanctis, PL* 156, cols 607–80.

8 Matthew Paris, *Chronica Majora*, ed. H. R. Luard, 7 vols (London, 1882–83).

9 *The Sayings of the Desert Fathers: The Alphabetical Collection* (Oxford and Kalamazoo, 1975), 41. Arsenius, p. 41.

10 Cf. James Bentley, *Restless Bones* (London, 1985), pp. 135–6.

11 Cf. Jean-Claude Schmitt, *The Holy Greyhound: Guinefort, Healer of Children since the Thirteenth Century* (Cambridge, 1983).

12 W. H. Anden, from the sequence 'Thanksgiving for a habitat', in *About the House* (New York, 1965; London, 1966).

13 Alexander Solzhenitsyn, *One Word of Truth* (London, 1972).

14 Dante, *The Divine Comedy*, Vol. III, *Paradise*, trans. Mark Musa (Harmondsworth, 1984), Canto 12, lines 23–4.

15 Dante, *Paradise*, Canto 12, lines 133, 137, 24.

16 Dante, *Paradise*, Canto XXXIII, line 145.

Bibliography

Translations used in this book

Quotations from the Bible are taken from the Authorized Version. Where no sources for other translations into English are given, they are mine.

All quotations from English translations of the works of Anselm are from *Anselm of Canterbury: The Major Works*, trans. Brian Davies and G. R. Evans, Oxford University Press, 1998, except the *Proslogion* and the *Prayers* and *Meditations* which are from *Prayers and Meditations of Saint Anselm with the Proslogion*, trans. Benedicta Ward, Harmondsworth, Penguin, 1973.

Select bibliography

Adams, Marilyn McCord, '*Fides Quaerens Intellectum*: St Anselm's Method in Philosophical Theology', *Faith and Philosophy*, Vol. 9, no. 4 (1992).

Anselm, *Sancti Anselmi Cantuariensis Archieposcopi, Opera Omnia*, ed. F. S. Schmitt, Edinburgh, Nelson, 1938–61.

Barth, Karl, *Anselm: Fides Quaerens Intellectum*, trans. Ian Robertson, Richmond, John Knox Press, 1960.

Cottier, Jean-François, *Anima mea: prières privées et textes de dévotion du Moyen Age latin*, Turnout, Brepols, 2002.

Davies, Brian and Leftow, Brian eds, *The Cambridge Companion to Anselm*, Cambridge University Press, 2004.

Eadmer, *Vita Sancti Anselmi*, trans. R. W. Southern as *The Life of St Anselm: Archbishop of Canterbury*, London, Thomas Nelson and Sons; Oxford University Press, 1962.

Eadmer, *Historia Novarum in Anglia*, trans. G. Bosanquet, London, Cresset Press, 1967.

Evans, Gillian Rosemary, *A Concordance to the Works of St. Anselm*, Millwood, NY, Kraus International Publications, 1984.

Evans, Gillian Rosemary, *Anselm*, Wilton, CT, Morehouse-Barlow, 1989.

Evans, Gillian Rosemary, *Anselm and a New Generation*, Oxford, Clarendon Press, 1980.

Evans, Gillian Rosemary, *Anselm and Talking about God*, New York, Oxford University Press, 1978.

Fortin, John, OSB (ed.), *Saint Anselm: His Origins and Influence*, Lewiston, NY, Edwin Mellen Press, 2001.

Hartshorne, Charles, *Anselm's Discovery*, La Salle, IL, Open Court, 1965.

Hick, John and McGill, Arthur C. (eds), *The Many-Faced Argument: Recent Studies on the Ontological Argument for the Existence of God*, New York, Macmillan, 1967.

Hopkins, Jasper, *A Companion to the Study of St. Anselm*, Minneapolis, University of Minnesota Press, 1972.

Letters of St Anselm, trans. Walter Fröhlich, Kalamazoo, MI, Cistercian Publications, 1990–1994, 3 vols.

McIntyre, J., *St. Anselm and His Critics: A Reinterpretation of Cur Deus Homo*, London and Edinburgh, Oliver and Boyd, 1954.

Patrologia Latina (PL), ed. J. P. Migne, 217 vols, Paris, 1844–55.

Plantinga, Alvin, *The Ontological Argument, from St. Anselm to Contemporary Philosophers*, Garden City, NY, Anchor Books, 1965.

Southern, R. W., *Saint Anselm: A Portrait in Landscape*, Cambridge University Press, 1990.

Southern, R. W., *Saint Anselm and His Biographer*, Cambridge University Press, 1963.

Relics

Benton, J. F. (ed.), *Self and Society in Medieval France: The Memoirs of Guibert of Nogent*, New York, 1970.

Bentley, James, *Restless Bones: The Story of Relics*, London, Constable, 1985.

Dooley, Eugene, *Church Law on Sacred Relics*, Washington, Catholic University of America, 1931.

Geary, Patrick, *Furta Sacra: The Theft of Relics in the Central Middle Ages*, Princeton, NJ, Princeton University Press, 1978.

Grabar, André, *Martyrium: recherches sur le culte des reliques et l'art chrétien antique*, 2 vols, Paris, 1946.

Herman-Mascard, N., *Les reliques des saints: formation coutumière d'un droit*, Paris, 1975.

Jones, C. W., *Saint Nicholas of Myra, Bari, and Manhattan: Biography of a Legend*, Chicago and London, University of Chicago Press, 1987.

Kemp, E. W., *Canonization and Authority in the Western Church*, London, Oxford University Press, 1948.

Schmitt, J.-C., *The Holy Greyhound: Guinefort, Healer of Children since the Thirteenth Century*, trans. Martin Thom, Cambridge University Press, 1983.

Ward, Benedicta, *Miracles and the Medieval Mind: Theory, Record and Event 1000–1215*, London, Scolar, 1982.

Woodruff, C. E. and Danks, W., *Memorials of Canterbury Cathedral*, London, 1912.

Index